UNDERSTANDING
AND TRAINING HORSES

UNDERSTANDING

AND TRAINING
HORSES

by A. James Ricci

Photographs by Joe Van Wormer

J. B. LIPPINCOTT COMPANY

PHILADELPHIA AND NEW YORK

CONTENTS

UNDERSTANDING AND TRAINING HORSES

1 / IN THE BEGINNING

In the following chapters I will try to teach you the principles involved in fine horsemanship, whether it be with grand dressage, Western pleasure, three-gaited, or reining horses. The methods I recommend are probably much different from other prescribed systems. Most of the techniques described have been worked out during a lifetime of study, devoted to not only the horse but all kinds of animals. I feel that the basic training for most divisions of the sport is the same and is aimed at controlling and understanding the horse.

The following chapters will not dwell on any specific division of the sport but on the sport in general. Regardless of what division of horsemanship you wish to finish in, the instructions to follow will assist you greatly in getting over the rough spots. Then you can, with minor adjustment, conform with the rules and regulations of any specific division.

I am writing these instructions fully realizing that there are conflicting opinions, expressed by many people, regarding stance, execution, position, balance, etc. What may be correct in one division would be incorrect in another. The reason for this is quite obvious. Many people do not recognize the fact that there is only one kind of horsemanship and that is *good* horsemanship. From its lowest form, the pleasure classes, to its highest form, grand dressage, the principles are the same. A well-schooled dressage horse would make an excellent reining horse and three-gaited horse, or even a good English or Western pleasure horse if his owner wished it; but he would have to make adjustments so that the horse conformed with the rules of the division. For instance, what would be considered a good stop in Western classes would be very crude in the dressage arena. By the same token, the stop used in the dressage arena would be frowned upon in a stock horse class. The adjustment in this case would pertain to balance. The rider should be able to control this movement either way, by adjusting his balance,

The controversial term "collection" is used in many divisions and has many different meanings. In dressage competitions it means a certain way of going, but it means a different way of going when used in connection with pleasure horses or three-gaited horses. The reason for this is that there are many levels of collection just as there are many levels of horsemanship.

So schooling a horse is a progressive thing, going from the lowest level to the highest level—the tests of the Grand Prix used in Olympic competitions. Regardless of the division the rider may choose or the level at which he wishes to stop, he should only feel that he has accomplished his purpose if he has a safe, quiet, obedient horse that works without restraint and with enough impulsion to get the job done. With these thoughts in mind, I have written this book.

Before we can talk of training the horse, we must first learn all we can about him. The horse is a creature that, standing on his hind legs, is almost twice the height of man. (Fig. 1) He weighs, in some cases, over five times as much as man and is also over ten times as powerful. He survived the various ice ages, as well as the age of dinosaurs and volcanoes, and during this time adapted himself to almost every climate and terrain.

FIG. 1

A Horse's Behavior

A horse is one of the oldest known animals on earth. His intelligence is based on his ability to survive. His ability to survive is based on how well he can protect himself. From close observations, I have found that a horse follows a definite behavior pattern for protection.

When he becomes frightened or alarmed, his skin and muscles become taut and he raises his head and neck high up and away from the point of danger. (Fig. 2) Tightening of the skin makes it more difficult for an assailant to bite or claw at him. His head, thrown up and away from the point of danger, insures protection to one of the most vulnerable spots of his body, the poll.

If the horse is attacked from the front, he rears up on his hind legs, keeping his head far above his attacker, and strikes out with his forelegs with pile-driving blows that would crush the skull of even the largest predatory animal. (Fig. 3)

Should an attack come from the rear, the horse would shift his weight to his front quarters and kick with a machine-gun-like rapidity that, if it did not kill, would soon discourage his assailant. (Fig. 4)

If attacked from the side, threatening flank and stomach, he pushes sideways into his attacker, quickly crushing him to the ground. If the attack comes from above, the horse will buck violently. As soon as his assailant is thrown to the ground, he will take off with a speed yet unmatched for his size. (Fig. 5)

The behavior pattern of a horse frightened or alarmed will be referred to as "Pattern A." "Pattern B" will describe the horse's actions while relaxed and passive.

If the horse, quietly grazing in his home pasture without any fear whatsoever, should suddenly prick his nose on a thorn from a nearby

Fig. 2 Frightened reaction.

Figs. 3, 4 Responses to attack from front and rear.

FIG. 5   Fleeing a thrown assailant.

bush, he would move his nose away from the annoyance, flexing his head at the poll, with the skin and muscles of his body relaxed. If a fly or a mosquito should light on his shoulder, he would reach around with his muzzle to remove it. Should this annoyance continue, he would not rear up and strike but would move his forequarters to one side. If a thorn should suddenly prick him on the hindquarters, he would not kick at it but simply move away from this bothersome pressure.

The point I'm trying to make is that the horse's reaction to annoyances when he is in a state of fear (Pattern A) is completely different from when he is relaxed and quiet (Pattern B). As a horse is a routinist, we must use a system of education that enables us to get the same reaction every time we wish it. The horse does not speak a language that we understand through hearing, but does have a language we can understand by observing: Pattern A and Pattern B.

With this knowledge of the horse, we create a language he will understand, one that is felt rather than spoken, so that the horse may learn about us. Since every foal, whether it be on the pampas of Argentina or in our own box stalls, does not know that it will grow up to carry man and do his bidding, he must be taught.

2 / TRAINING THE COLT

Training should start two weeks after the foal is born. Older horses can also be trained by this system of education; but the older the horse, the greater the problems you will encounter, as many bad habits may be well established. However, if the horse has been previously taught by methods similar to those used here, training will go much easier.

A young foal that has never been in contact with man looks at him with distrust and inquisitiveness, staying his distance, yet curious enough to come closer. (Fig. 6)

When he comes to you, handle him gently but firmly, enclosing his entire body with your arms. (Fig. 7) He may struggle, but under no circumstances should you allow him to go free while he is still struggling.

He has suddenly realized he is being restricted and will revert to Pattern A. He will try to kick, paw, buck, and crowd, with his head and nose straight up in the air. Speaking to him all the time, you can finally subdue him and make him passive. Only when he is quiet and passive should you turn him loose.

You have now made the greatest impression that will ever be made on the colt's mind during his entire life. That is, even though he was restricted, no harm came to him. Repeat this procedure as often as possible, making sure that the foal does not become injured

18

FIGS. 6, 7, 8, 9   Getting acquainted with the colt.

in any way during this delicate and important part of his training. Soon the foal will be coming to you without fear or distrust and will be handled without any reversion to Pattern A.

You should be able to flex his head and neck and bend it from one side to the other without his muscles becoming stiff or hard. (Fig. 8)

You can lead him around with just your hand over his neck by tapping him slightly from behind with a short buggy whip. (Fig. 9)

LEADING

The colt is now ready for the halter. After the halter has been placed about the colt's head and properly adjusted, with halter shank snapped in place, stand on the near side, the colt's left side, approximately at his shoulder, facing in the same direction as the colt with the halter lead in your right hand. You should have a short buggy

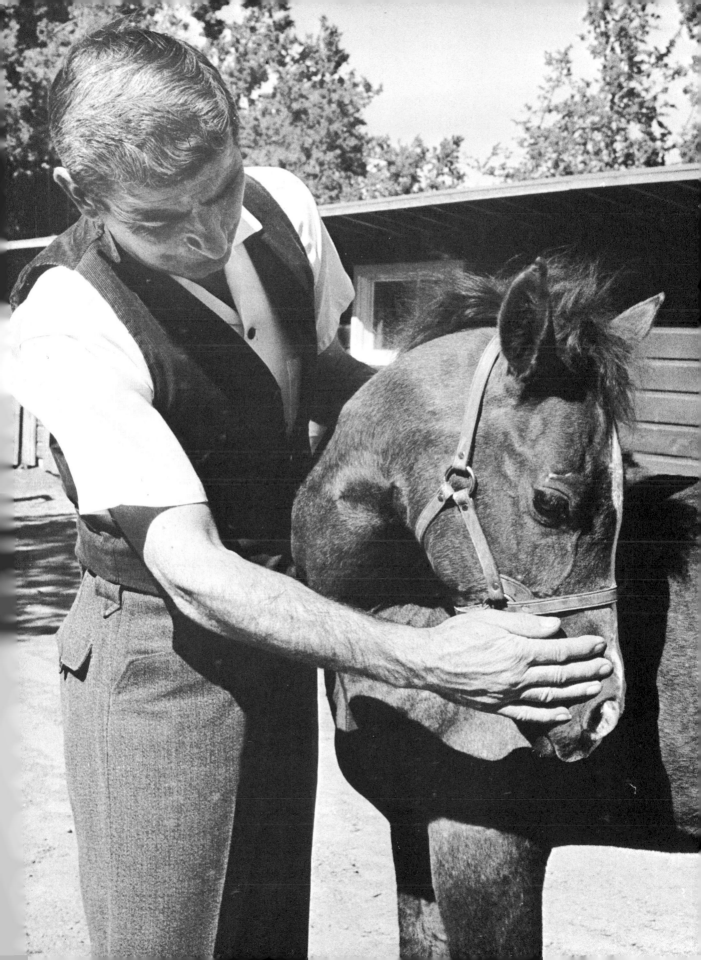

Fig. 9

whip in your left hand, with the handle pointing in the direction in which you are facing. With your right hand, push at the colt's withers and say, "Come on," or any other phrase you desire to use when you ask the colt to move on. (Fig. 10)

Figs. 10, 11, 12   Leading the colt.

Fig. 11

Probably nothing will happen as the colt does not understand your language, so a quick tap with the buggy whip at the colt's hocks will move him forward. (Fig. 11) However, only use the whip if the colt fails to respond to the voice command. Once or twice the whip may be necessary before the colt will obey, but it may never have to be used again if this first lesson of obedience has been executed properly. (Fig. 12)

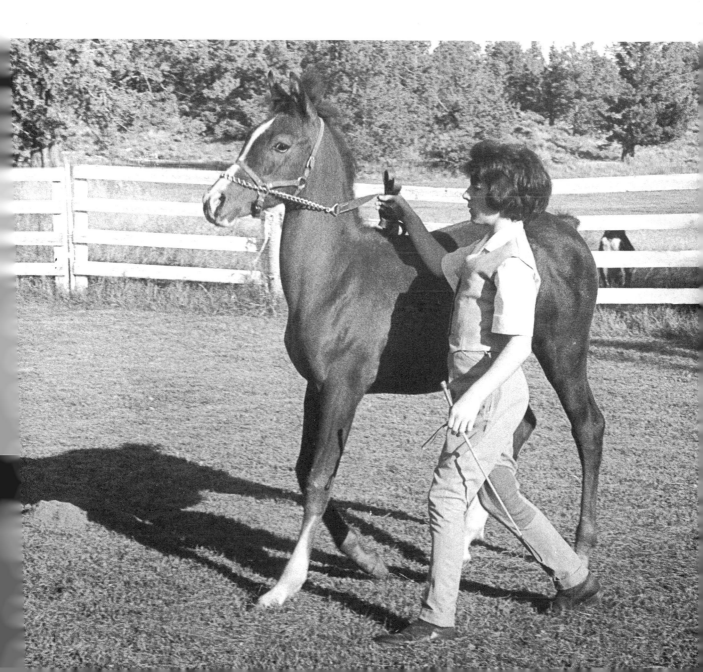

STOPPING

Now you should be leading the colt. The next procedure follows logically. You must teach the colt to stop when you ask him to. You point the lash of the buggy whip in the direction in which you are moving, carrying it slightly ahead of the colt's chest. You give the command, "Whoa," and stop moving. The noseband of the halter will tighten on the colt's nose. At the same time, tap the colt with the buggy whip just above the knees. (Fig. 13) For a second the colt may revert to Pattern A, as the attack is coming from the front. He will throw his weight on his hindquarters in order to be able to strike with his forequarters. This lightens his front end. You must remember to tap only once or else the colt may rear. As soon as this command has been executed, drop the whip and fondle the colt, placing his muzzle under your arm, and relax the muscles of his neck by massaging. When muscles are relaxed and the head is flexible, you know that the colt is quiet and passive.

HANDLING THE COLT

It is important that the colt knows you mean him no harm and that he permits much handling without becoming frightened. You will now examine the colt's weapons. As described in Pattern A, while the colt is under the influence of fear, his forefeet and hind feet can be thought of as weapons.

With the colt standing quietly, massage from the shoulder to the knee and from the knee to the fetlock, pressing with your index finger and thumb, with the palm of your hand cupped around the cannon

FIG. 13 Stopping the colt.

bone. You will find that pressure on one particular spot will cause the colt to pick up his feet. (Fig. 14) Hold his foot firmly for a few seconds and then place it back on the ground. (Fig. 15) Now go to the neck and head, massage and flex. If flexion is evident, and the skin on his neck is loose, the colt is still in the area of Pattern B.

Now, massage down the back, over the hip, down the flank, across the stifle to the buttocks. (Figs. 16 and 17) If the colt does not crowd or push toward you, continue to the hock down the cannon bone to the fetlock. (Fig. 18) The colt may fidget a little, but if he does not crowd into you, he is still in the area of Pattern B.

Now pick up the colt's hind leg. (Fig. 19) Immediately step back so that if the colt tries to kick, his thrust will be very weak. (Fig. 20) *Repeat this on the opposite side, as whatever is done on one side must be repeated on the other side.*

I recommend leading from both sides alternately. This should eventually help in developing control as well as in developing the colt's muscles evenly. So far the colt's education covers being handled, led, and stopped with a halter on, and allowing you to pick up all four of his feet. Each time you work with your colt, repeat these lessons until they become well established in his mind.

THE THREE MASTER CONTROLS

For this step in his training we should consider the colt as though he were divided into three sections, with the head and neck one section, the hindquarters a second section, and the forequarters a third. Referring back to Pattern A, the horse, in his endeavors to protect himself, instinctively divides his body into three areas of defense that correspond to these three sections. You have learned that, while retaining the colt's respect for your authority, you must passively control these three sections.

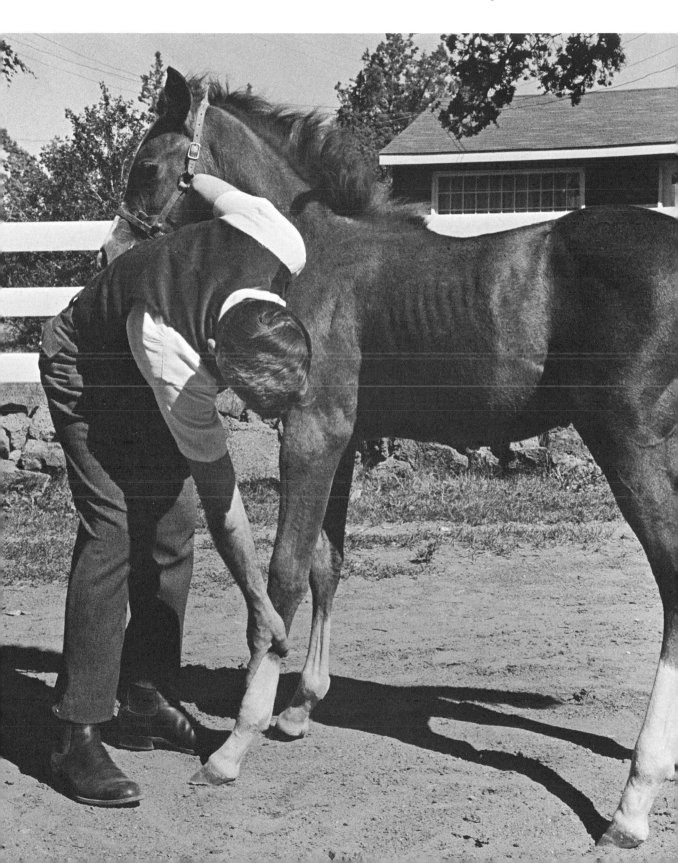

FIGS. 14, 15, 16, 17, 18, 19, 20   Handling the colt.

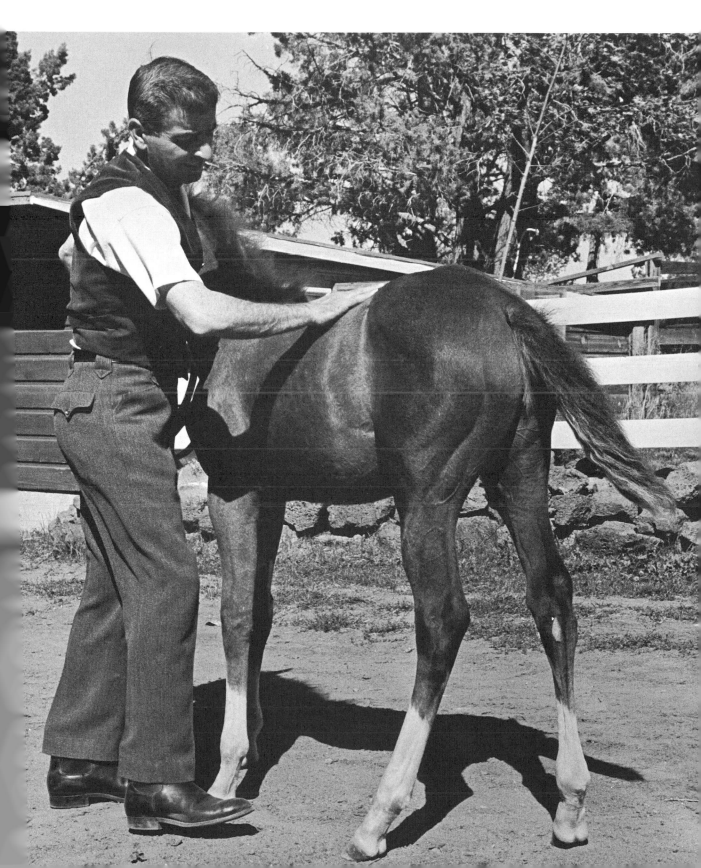

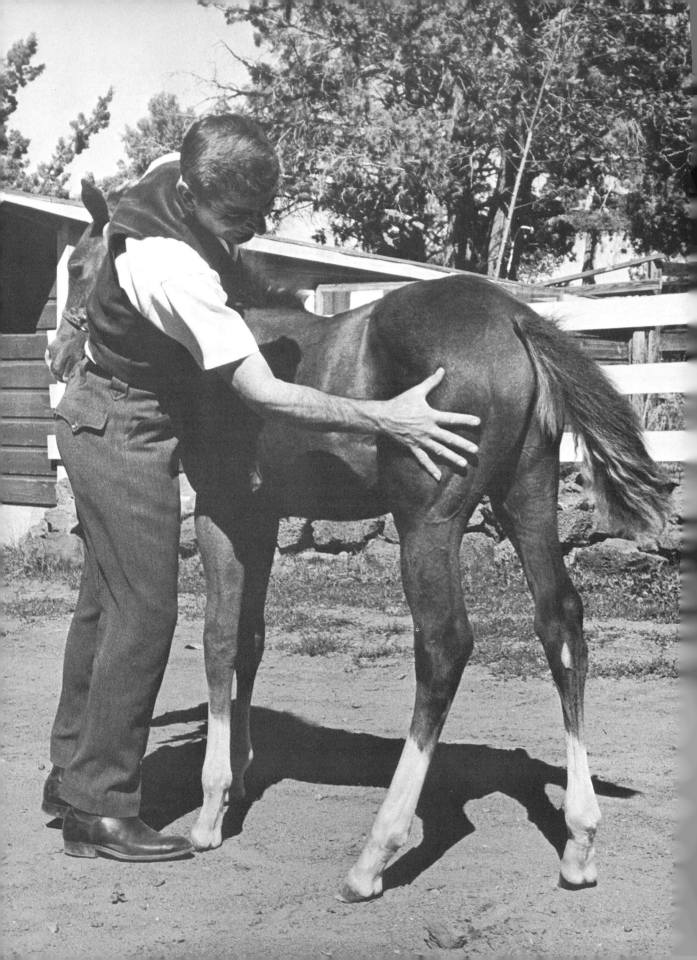

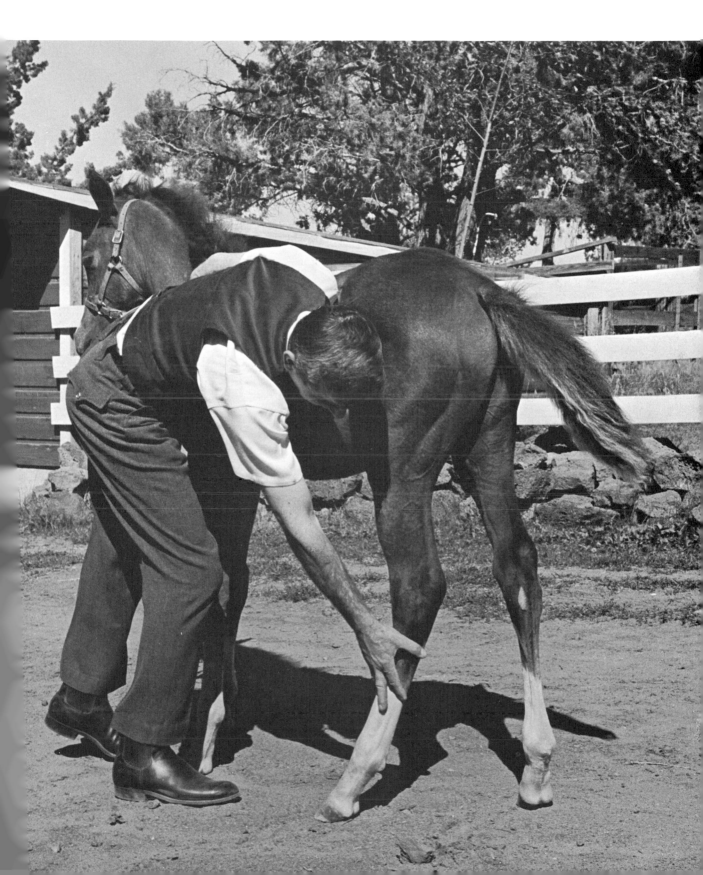

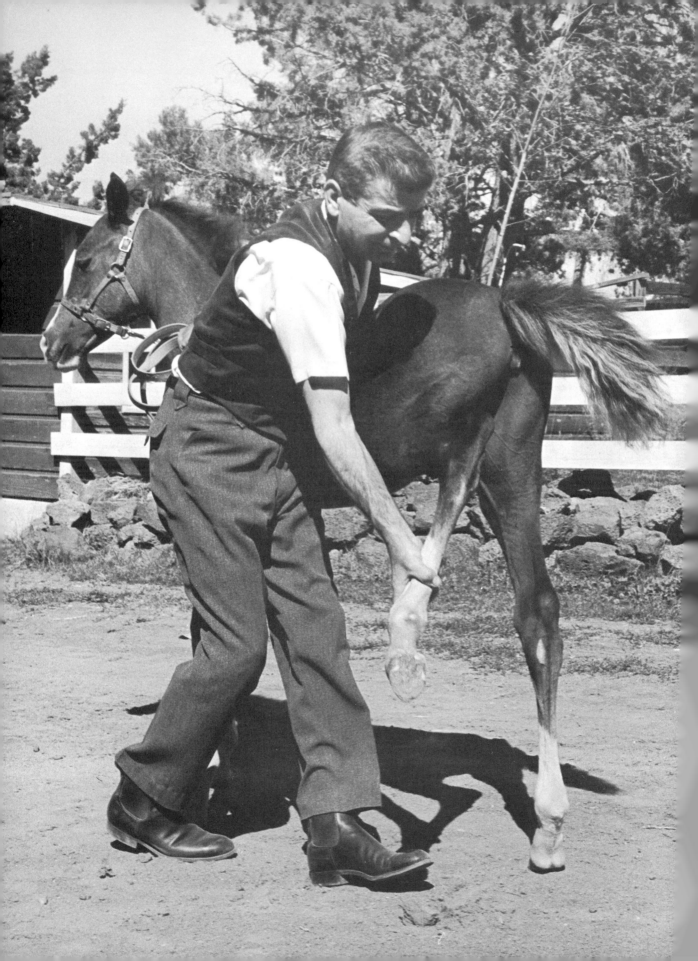

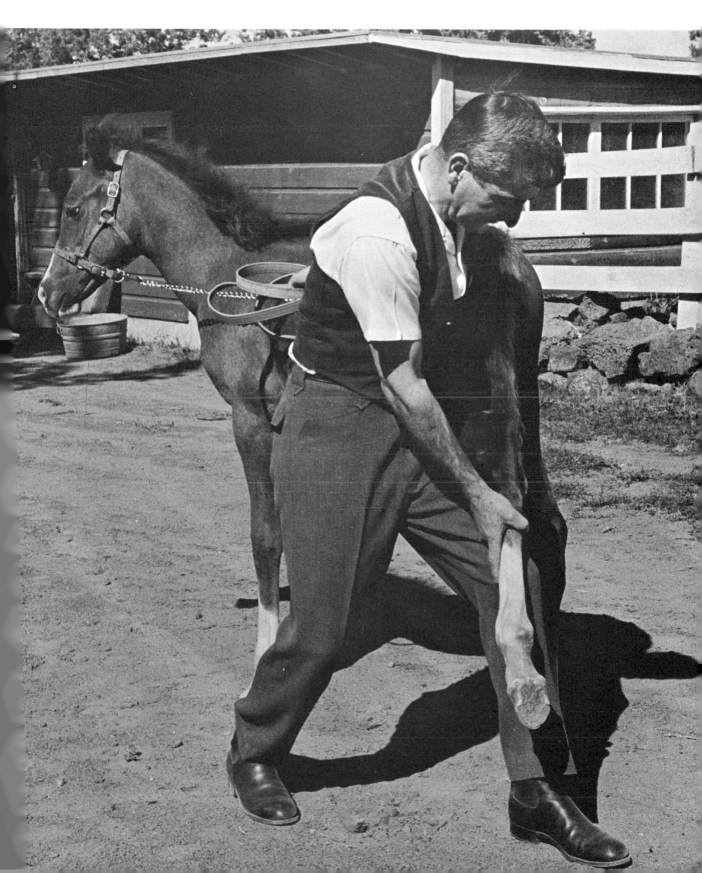

You should begin with the head and neck. Use a small chain similar to the ones used in training dogs, approximately eighteen inches long with a ring at each end. The chain is placed over the colt's nose with each end going through the halter ring and connected below by a halter lead. This is similar to the desert hackamore used centuries ago. To prevent the chain from slipping down over the colt's nose, tie a piece of string around the chain at the bridge of the nose and fasten it above, either to the colt's forelock or to the crown piece of the halter. (Fig. 21) The colt will not object to the chain since he has already been taught to flex his head with the halter.

He must now be taught to follow your hand. By pulling gently on the halter shank and guiding his muzzle with the other hand, attempt to bring his head around so that his nose will touch his shoulder. (Fig. 22) A slight pull on the chain below the chin causes a downward pressure on the bridge of the nose, thus bringing the nose down and creating flexion from the poll. (Fig. 23) An upward pressure of the chain against the lower jaw causes the colt to move his head away from this pressure and results in an upward movement of the head. (Fig. 24) This must be done on both sides. Much caution must be taken so that you do not jerk or pull too hard. Gently and persistently this should be done along with the other lessons being taught. The purpose of following the hand will be more evident as training progresses.

Next in importance is the control of the hindquarters. By standing on the near side and facing the colt broadside, with the halter lead in your left hand and a short buggy whip in your right, press the colt's side with your right hand approximately eight to ten inches behind where the cinch (girths) will ultimately go. This pressure should be strong enough to be of an annoying nature, but no sharp instrument should be used that would suddenly startle the colt or cause him to revert to Pattern A. In Pattern A, you will remember, an attack from the side would cause the colt to push into you, which would be

Fig. 21   Proper adjustment of chain and halter.

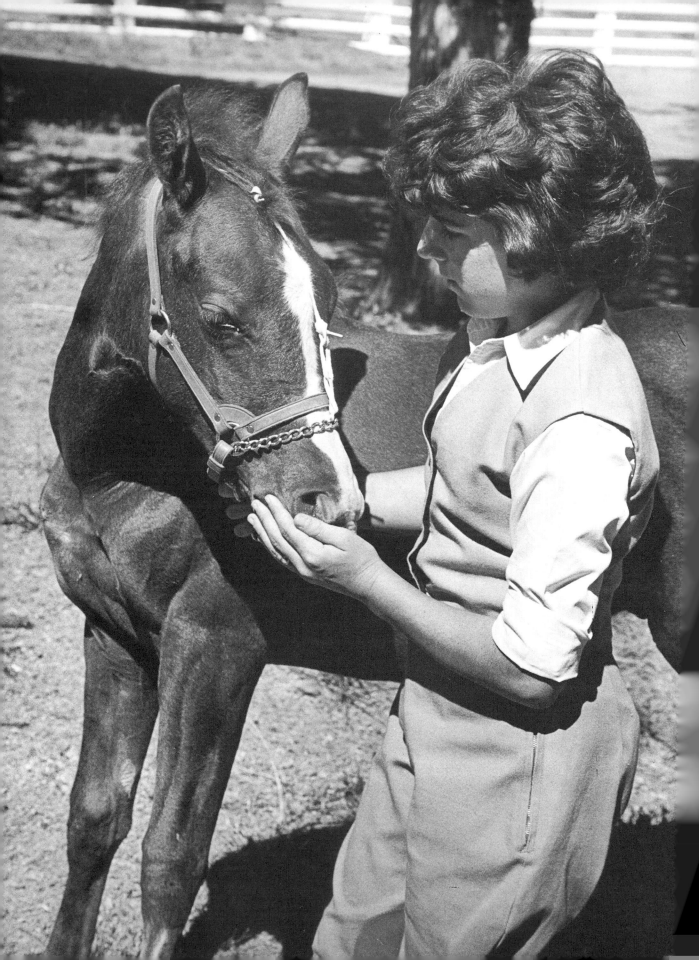

FIGS. 22, 23, 24 Control of the neck and head.

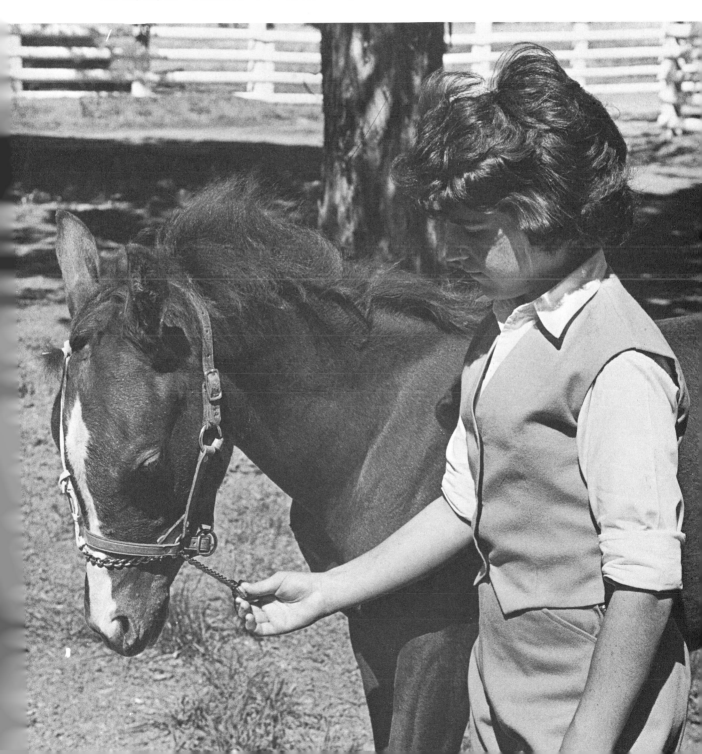

Fig. 25 Control of the hindquarters. [*Note: White crosses in this and subsequent photographs indicate points to which touch or pressure should be applied.*]

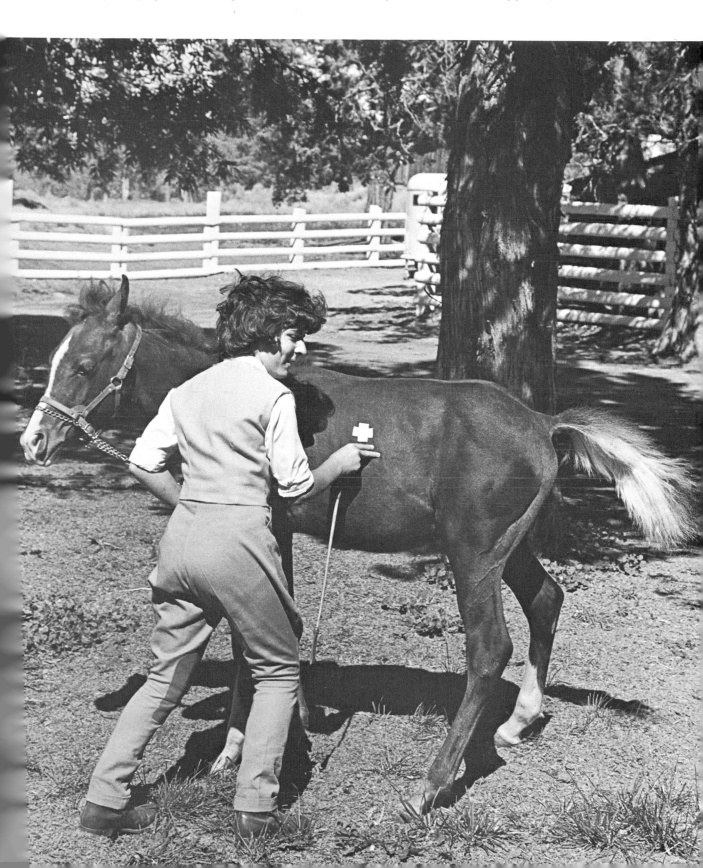

just the opposite of what you are trying to establish. Watch, then, for the danger signal. If the colt does not move away from the pressure and does not crowd into you, a quick tap on the hock, as well as increased pressure, will cause the hindquarter to move away while the forequarter remains on the spot. If only one or two steps are accomplished, immediately throw the whip to the ground and once again fondle the colt and flex the head. (Fig. 25)

Again the pressure is exerted. Now, maybe three or four steps can be gained. Continue this process until the colt has gone around his forequarters in a complete circle; then repeat the exercise in the opposite direction. This is known as the control of the hindquarter or the pivot on the forehand.

Now go to the third section. This is known as the control of the forequarters or the pivot on the haunches. (Fig. 26) Stand on the near side of the colt, facing in the same direction as he does, with your right hand holding the halter lead in line with the colt's shoulder. Be extremely careful not to touch the colt at this stage of the training, except when giving him a command to execute or when fondling him. Never command and fondle him at the same time.

Your left hand holds the short buggy whip. With your right hand press against the colt's shoulder—not steadily but intermittently, gradually increasing the annoyance. (Fig. 27) If the colt does not move one step within a few seconds, cease the pressure. Hold the whip in a position so that when the right hand again starts to press against the shoulder, you can tap the whip alternately on the side of the colt's muzzle and knee. The colt should begin to revert to Pattern A, throwing his weight on his hindquarter. This will cause him to take one or two steps away from you. You have now established some respect for the pressure against the shoulder. Stop and caress the colt. Flex his neck and return his behavior to Pattern B. Continue with this procedure until, without the use of the whip, the colt will move away from the pressure of the hand against his shoulder.

It is probable that while working with the colt's front quarters the hindquarters have been somewhat neglected. It may be that when the colt takes one step away from you with his forequarters, he is also taking one step toward you with his hindquarters—in other words, doing a turn on the center which you do not want. If this is the case, take advantage of the colt's balance. Before asking him to move his forequarters away from you, take the halter lead in your left hand and bring his head around toward you six to eight inches off center. His head is now in such a position that it will restrict his hindquarters from moving toward you.

Press against the colt's shoulder, and he should commence to do

FIGS. 26, 27 Control of the forequarters.

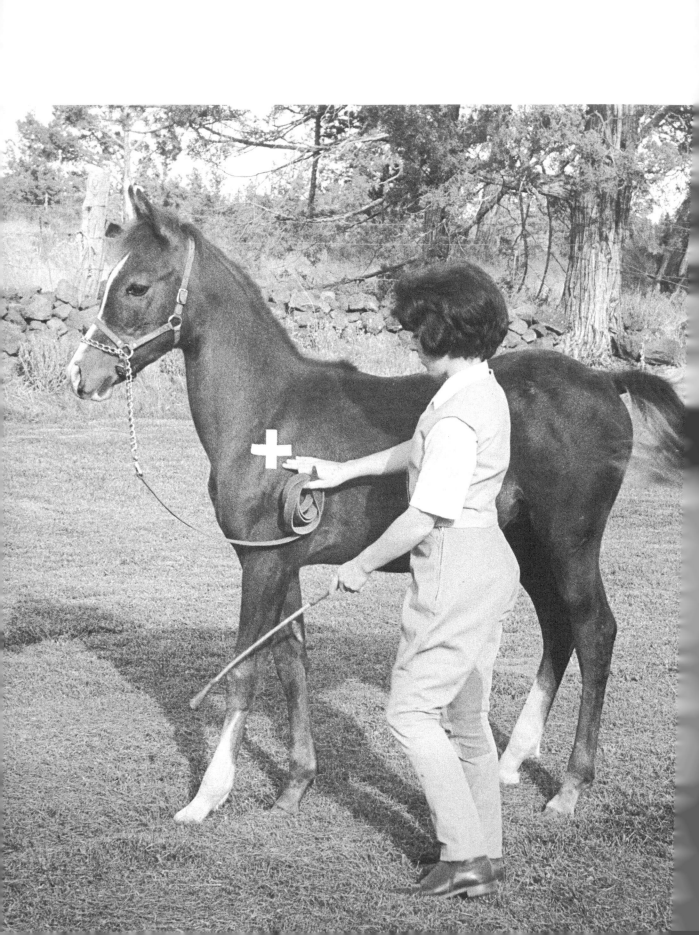

the pivot on the haunches correctly. This exercise must also be repeated on both sides. When the pressure on the shoulder has been well established and the colt will make a complete circle around his hindquarters quickly and without fear, you have gained a most important control: the basis for the turn from you while he is in motion.

These three controls must be mastered. The more you practice, the quicker the colt will respond. The importance of these controls, executed precisely in the manner described, will soon become evident and cannot be overemphasized.

THE STOP AND TURN

Stand beside the colt on the near side, facing the same direction as the colt. Hold the halter shank in your right hand and the whip in your left hand. Start the colt moving forward for a distance of fifteen to twenty feet. (Fig. 28) Now bring the colt to a stop. As soon as the colt has stopped, press against his shoulder and move his front quarter around while he pivots on the haunches until he is heading in the direction from which he started. (Fig. 29) This exercise must be repeated over and over on both sides.

PRACTICE OF THE PIVOTS

When the three basic controls and the stop and turn appear to be mastered, it is time to ask for more accuracy.

Until now, nothing has been mentioned about which foot should remain anchored while the pivots are being executed. Actually, it didn't make a great deal of difference in the beginning, as control of the quarters was more important. Now, however, it is important to

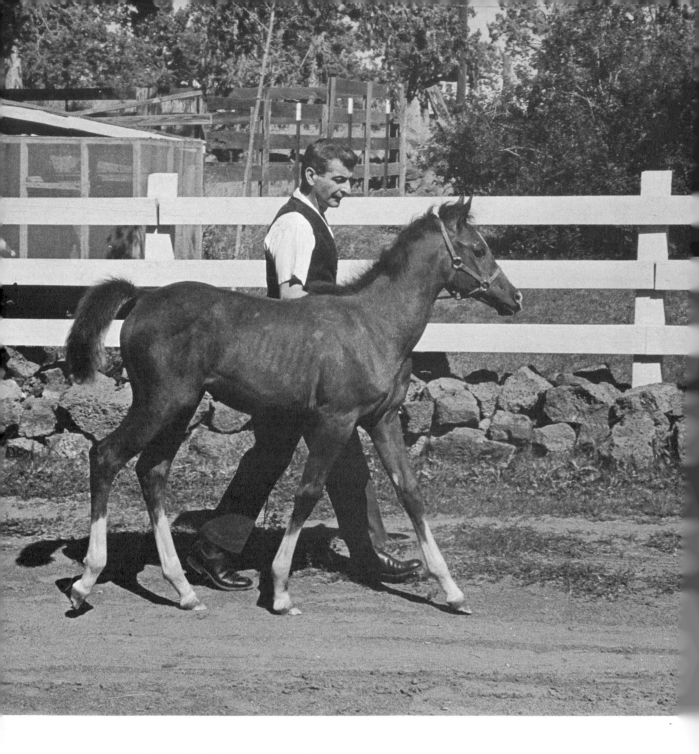

FIGS. 28, 29   Turning the colt.

stress holding the correct leg for proper balance. In the control of the hindquarter, which is also the pivot on the forehand, the colt should hold the front leg on the side against which the pressure is being exerted. If the colt picks up his front feet as though marking time while doing a pivot on the forehand, give a quick jerk on the halter lead and proceed to do so any time he does this. Soon he will realize you want him to hold one foot. When using the control of the forequarter, which results in a pivot on the haunches, you want the colt to hold one hind leg anchored on the side that he turns into.

For example, if the pressure is exerted against his left shoulder, he should hold his right hind leg or vice versa. If you watch closely, you will notice that, if you back the colt slightly while he executes a pivot on the haunches, he will hold the wrong foot. If you pull forward slightly while he is executing the pivot, he will hold the correct foot. Consequently, do not back the colt at all while he is executing a pivot on the haunches or he will pivot on the wrong foot and be off balance. This will hamper his endeavors to become a good reining horse.

When the colt is moving away from the slightest touch both fore and hind, and also following the hand well with the halter lead and noseband, you are ready for the next important exercise, which will teach the colt to stand still and enable you to control the quarters from a distance.

The pivot on the haunches done slowly from either a standstill or from a walk requires a different balance from that of the fast turn or the rollback. The balance of the fast turn differs in that the horse places the bulk of his weight on the opposite hind leg from the side he turns on and uses his other hind leg to help propel him around. The horse does this to cushion his momentum so that all his weight won't pile up on the side that is making the turn. To give you a better illustration, try this experiment yourself. Walk slowly a distance of about ten feet, stop, turn to the left holding one foot on the spot. Notice that invariably this foot will be your left foot if you make the turn slowly. Now try it again, walking rapidly for ten feet. Stop quickly, turning to your left, holding one foot in place as you turn, and invariably you will find that the foot you hold will be your right. The horse will switch feet as he speeds up; however, if he is moving slowly, the horse will hold the leg on the side he turns toward.

3 / CONTROL OF THE HORSE FROM A DISTANCE

In order to start these exercises, you need a longe line ten to twelve feet long and a buggy whip eight to ten feet long. First, position the colt broadside, holding the line in the left hand and the whip in the right, and face his near side. Now, attempt to walk backwards, away from the colt while he remains stationary. If he tries to follow, a quick jerk on the longe line should stop him. As soon as you can hold the colt still from a distance of ten feet, while facing him broadside, try to make him respond to the control of the fore and hindquarters with the touch of the buggy whip.

A quick tap on the colt's side should move his hindquarters away so that the colt is now facing you. (Fig. 30) A quick tap on the shoulder should move his forequarter away so that he is again broadside. (Fig. 31) This should be repeated on both sides.

Once again place the colt broadside. Back away ten feet while holding the rope in your left hand and the whip in your right, and face the near side of the colt. With a quick tap on the hocks, set the colt in motion. (Fig. 32) If the colt tries to head in facing you, a quick tap on the shoulder should straighten him out so that he will move around you in a circle.

You should have now, without exciting the colt, established control of his quarters from a distance. In this case the colt will be longeing the first time you try it without any difficulty whatsoever. (Fig. 33)

50

FIGS. 30, 31 Control of the fore and hindquarters with the buggy whip.

Fig. 31

FIGS. 32, 33   Longeing the colt.

Fig. 33

This also must be done in both directions. When you wish the colt to stop, a quick tap on the forelegs in conjunction with a quick jerk of the rope and the command "whoa" will stop him. Soon only the voice will be necessary.

These are the same controls that were first used in a stationary position, then while the colt was in motion, and now with the colt some distance away. In all cases the controls are the same. In each phase of training it is most important that these controls be mastered.

BACKING UP

Now it is time to teach the colt to back up. You do so by standing in front of the colt and giving the command, "Back up," accompanied by a series of taps on both forearms of the colt. (Fig. 34) This should set him in motion backwards. Be careful not to excite the colt with too much tapping as this might cause him to revert to Pattern A, and he will prepare to defend himself from an attack in front by rearing up and pawing with his front feet. You must constantly be on the alert for the danger signals that by now should be well established in your mind.

FIG. 34   Backing the colt.

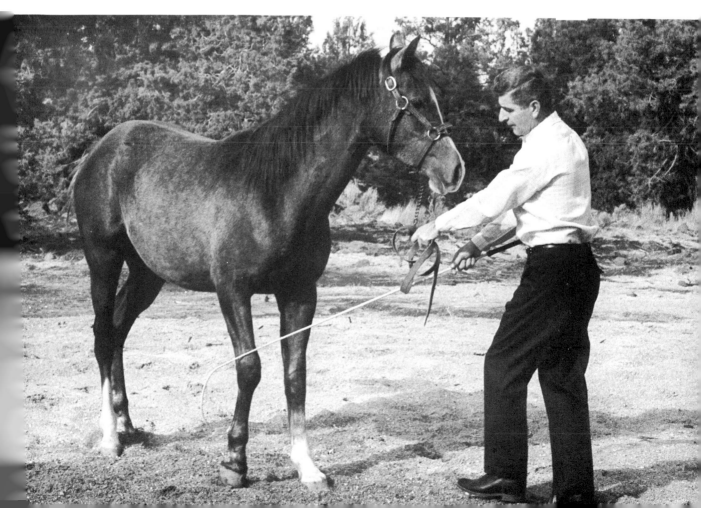

FIRST STEPS TO DRIVING

With the colt working well in both directions on the longe line, go one step further. Instead of standing in the center of the circle, with the colt going around, step toward the colt and slightly to his rear. Move closer and closer until the longe line is nearly parallel to the colt's side and you are following the colt around almost in his own tracks. (Fig. 35) What you will actually be doing is driving the colt with one line. (Fig. 36) This, of course, must be done on both sides.

FIGS. 35, 36   First steps to driving the colt.

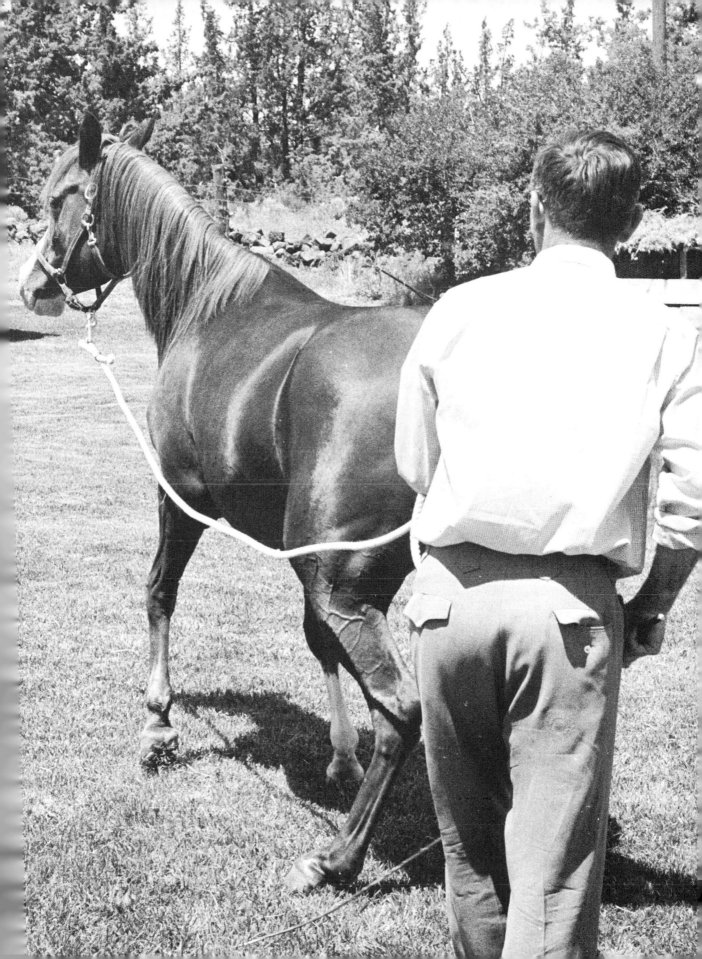

A Lesson in Obedience

It would be well, at this time, to teach the colt to come to you, as there are instances, such as leading through narrow places and loading in a trailer, when you will have to be in front of the colt and call him to you. The best method is to stand directly in front of him with the chain over his nose and with a lead rope about ten or twelve feet long. With a series of quick jerks on the rope, use the word command, "Come here." This may cause a reverse action at first, and the colt will try to back up. Do not give any ground unless the colt tries to rear. Gently, but persistently, cause the colt to step toward you. If this is accomplished without any help and without the use of the whip, you will never have any trouble loading him in a trailer. In fact, he should come to you on voice command alone. Also, he should never pull at the halter rope when tied. I realize this system of calling the colt to you is in direct opposition to what most trainers prescribe. However, I have always used this method and have never had any trouble loading horses alone. You caress the colt to show him your appreciation.

The Lesson of the Bit

An important step in the colt's life is his introduction to the bit when he is at least one year old or older. The measure of your success in introducing him to the bit may well determine whether you can advance to a higher plane of horsemanship or will remain in a mediocre class. Begin by placing a snaffle bit in the colt's mouth. Then attach the rings of the bit to part of the halter with short pieces of string or rawhide, still using the halter with the chain over the colt's nose to control him. After the colt has worn the bit for at least three weeks, he will be ready to receive the lesson of the bit. Before you teach it to him, you yourself should have a thorough understanding of this lesson.

To start with, you know that when the chain you have been using creates pressure against the bridge of the colt's nose, he will lower his muzzle, tuck in slightly, or, in other words, will flex at the poll. A pressure of the chain against the lower jaw from underneath will cause the colt to raise his head. A pressure on one side of his muzzle will cause him to move in the opposite direction—away from the pressure. These facts have already been established, and now with the introduction of the bit, nothing will be changed except that the bit will allow you to use the head and neck to balance the colt.

Between the front teeth and the grinders of the lower jaw you will notice that there are two bare places, one on each side. These are known as the bars of the mouth. With the bit lying on top of the tongue, a slight pressure of the rein will bring the bit in contact with the bars, thus causing the same reaction as the chain created with pressure on the bridge of the nose. Now, if you slide the bit up to the corners of the colt's mouth, a slight pressure of the rein will cause the same reaction as would a chain below the chin, and, of course, this causes the head to be raised. If both reins are brought to one side, the pressure against the colt's jaw will create the same reaction as did the chain against the side of the muzzle. So you see it isn't the type of bit used that creates different reactions, but where the pressure is brought to bear. If these pressures become too great, the colt will again revert to Pattern A and throw his head up, and, temporarily, all will be lost. So you must take care only to worry the head down and not jerk or pull it down. I might add at this time that I do not recommend tie-downs or bitting rigs to set the colt's head in the proper position.

SETTING THE HEAD AND DRIVING WITH ELEMENTARY COLLECTION

The best way to establish the correct position for the colt to carry his head is to teach him balance of his entire body, which can be done by driving him. For equipment you will need a bridle with snaffle bit only, a circingle with two side rings, and a piece of half-inch cotton or nylon rope, approximately thirty feet long, with a snap hook on each end.

With the circingle cinched up and the colt bridled, snap one end of the rope in the ring of the bit, then pass the other end of the rope through the ring on the circingle on the same side affixed to the bit. Now go over the colt's back, through the other ring of the circingle, and fasten the end of the rope to the ring of the bit. This provides enough rope to drive the colt, and you will still be back far enough so that if the colt should kick, you will be in the clear. Start the colt driving on one rein only, in the same manner as that used in longeing him. (Fig. 37) Soon you will be able to walk directly in back of him. Be careful not to turn him sharply as he is not acquainted with turning from the pull of the rein; so you should use the buggy whip to tap the quarters and guide him with the system with which he is familiar. Soon, just the slightest touch of the rein against his sides will cause him to turn.

When the colt is turning well and is not afraid of being driven, it is time to teach him to walk and trot with his hind legs well under his body. This is done by an intermittent tapping with the buggy whip on the colt's hocks. Soon he will be working with his legs well under him. But because of your presence behind him and the worrying of the hind legs with the whip, the colt may partially revert to Pattern A. As you remember, when an attack comes from the rear, a horse throws his weight on his forequarters and prepares to defend himself from behind if necessary. This is exactly what has happened. Even though the colt's hind legs are well under his body, he is heavy in front, carrying his head low, and is not balanced. (Fig. 38)

ESTABLISHING BALANCE

The next procedure is to correct this undesirable position by using two more pieces of equipment: an overcheck bit and a crupper. The overcheck is a small snaffle bit that is placed in the colt's mouth,

FIGS. 37, 38 Driving the colt.

with a strap going up over the head and down the neck, fastening to the circingle. If the equipment is properly adjusted, it will raise the head and neck because the pressure of the bit will be brought against the corners of the colt's mouth.

The crupper goes around the base of the tail to connect with the circingle. This keeps the circingle from pulling forward when the overcheck is being used. Now, with the neck up and the head flexed, and the hind legs well under his body, the colt is truly balanced and collected.

You should continue to drive him in this manner as he is not old enough to ride, but you should practice all the colt has learned for a period of fifteen to thirty minutes each day—handling his feet, follow-

Fig. 38

ing the hand, the pivots, longeing, driving, etc. If it takes longer than thirty minutes to review all that has been learned, split it up into two sessions, doing half one day and half another.

The colt may lay his ears back and shake his head or wring his tail; he may be sick, tired, or just plain angry. Whatever the cause, you should discontinue working him until it no longer exists. When you start working him again, do it in the presence of other horses, if possible, since a temporary distraction could ease the monotony of the lessons until you can do exercises that are more fun for him.

AUXILIARY AIDS

By this time the colt will be somewhat of a specialist at what he has mastered, and he is also beginning to develop some of the necessary muscles needed to carry a rider when the time comes. With his third birthday approaching, you should begin to prepare him for the saddle.

In conjunction with the three aids or controls we have learned from the ground, there are a few auxiliary aids that have not been mentioned. These are voice commands such as: "Whoa," "Back up," "Come on," "Come here," and "Hold." You will now supplement the five words with two more, "Pick up," and "Under," making a total of seven words which will complete our verbal commands for the time being. Although some horses can understand over fifty distinct words, you ask for only seven.

Place the colt broadside wearing a halter with the chain over his nose in the same manner as in his preliminary training. Stand facing his near side, holding the halter lead in your left hand and the buggy whip in your right. First, raise the colt's head and neck, keeping him well flexed. Give the command, "Pick up," and tap the colt behind the knee of the near forefoot. This should cause him to step forward one step. Then, again giving the command, "Pick up," and reaching under the horse, tap the forefoot on the off side behind the knee, and he should step forward one step. If the colt moves his hind legs, reprimand him by shaking the halter lead and giving the command, "Hold." It should not be difficult to make him hold his hind legs as he will already hold any one leg we wish him to.

Progressively, we cause him to step forward far enough so that he will be stretched and in a state of *extension*. (Fig. 39) I realize that some horse show rules do not allow a horse to stretch in the show ring, but it is simply an exercise to prepare the colt for the saddle.

Fig. 39   Extended position.

After the colt has stretched so that his front legs are four to six inches before vertical (vertical being a position when both fore and hind cannon bones are perpendicular), allow him to hold his position for only a few seconds.

With the lead rope in your left hand and facing the colt's near side, lower his head slightly, giving the command, "Under," and, at the same time, tap both hocks with the buggy whip. This should eventually cause the colt to place his legs well under his body. (Fig. 40) So we go from an extended position to a collected position, and the two positions will have a direct bearing on his ability to perform under saddle. If the colt moves forward, we will lose the effect, so reprimand him and keep his front legs firm. Soon, use of the words "pick up" and "under" alone will cause the colt to extend and collect.

FIG. 40   Collected position.

After two or three weeks of executing this exercise, it will become apparent what kind of working horse you will have. If the colt does well in extension but not so well in collection, it means that possibly you have a standing-behind horse. If the colt collects well but has trouble in extending or stretching, you then have a standing-under type of horse. If the colt can extend and collect well, you truly have a versatile animal.

4 / EVALUATING THE COLT

A T THIS STAGE of the colt's training we should be concerned with his conformation. To examine this condition a little closer, have the horse standing broadside with both cannon bones—fore and hind—perpendicular. If the horse has a level croup, the back side of the cannon bone and the hind leg should line up with the point of the buttocks. If the horse is standing behind, this point will fall far short of lining up with the buttocks. If the point is two or three inches into the buttocks, he will be a standing-under type.

MEASUREMENTS OF AN IDEAL HORSE

After many years of study and observation of the bone structure of the versatile type of horse—one that can deliver maximum extension as well as collection regardless of his height—I have found a definite way of measuring the qualities looked for in the ideal horse. The horse must have reached his height and must be fairly well muscled. He must have a level croup, straight legs, long sloping pasterns, and a shoulder of approximately forty-five degrees which should automatically place his withers in the proper place. The rest of the horse can actually be measured as follows: The distance from the highest point of the center of the withers to the ground should be approximately the same as the distance from the point of the shoulder to the base of the tail. This measurement would be the same as that from the center of the withers up the neck, between the ears, down the face to the lower part of the muzzle. In other words, a versatile horse is as long as he is tall, and has a neck of the same length which enables him to reach the ground for food and water without bending his knees. The distance from the center of the withers to the point of the shoulder should approximate that from the point of the shoulder

FIGS. 41, 42   A well conformed horse.

to the center of the knee. The distance from the point of the shoulder to the point of the elbow should equal the distance from the point of the elbow to the center of the knee, as well as that from the center of the knee to the ground at the heel of his forefoot. (Figs. 41, 42) From the point of the hock to the heel of the hind foot should be the same distance as from the point of the hock to the center of the stifle joint, which in turn should measure the same as the distance from the center of the stifle joint to the hip and from the hip to the base of the tail. If the horse is so porportioned, his limbs are in proper alignment, so that all that is asked of him in extension and collection can be achieved with practice.

I realize these measurements will vary, but the closer we get to the previously described alignments, the better the results will be. With this information, it should not be too difficult to determine what type horse you have, so you can train accordingly. If the horse is a standing-behind type, he can never be a top reining animal and will not go well in three-gaited or dressage work, as he will be physically incapable of doing collected movements. If the horse is a standing-under type, he can do well in reining, games, calf roping and cutting, but he will be restricted in trotting or distance racing because he is physically incapable of a great amount of extension. If the horse is straight-legged and balanced, he will be able to accomplish any feat of horsemanship if you continue with this method of training.

5 / PRELIMINARY SADDLE TRAINING

You have now reached the point most of you have been waiting for. You are ready to ride the colt. With the colt saddled and bridled, wearing a snaffle bit and regular riding rein, check and make sure that the colt is relaxed by flexing and bending his neck. You should have the colt in a compound or corral, so that if anything should go wrong, he cannot go far. Of course, you should do all that you can to prevent a mishap, as an accident at this time may slow your progress considerably. You must be sure that in no way will the colt be suddenly frightened from unexpected sources.

When all is well, with the use of a mounting block you mount and sit quietly, with your feet out of the stirrups. The top tread of the stirrup should come to your ankle bone. (Fig. 43) If stirrup length is correct, place your feet in the stirrups. The colt should stand quietly, as he is used to you and has been handled long enough so that sitting on his back should not excite him. If he should become excited, his neck will stiffen. Recall Pattern A: if an attack comes from above, the colt will buck violently. So you must watch for this danger signal.

Now it is quite evident that a certain position must be assumed in the saddle in order to use the controls you have learned from the ground. With your heels down, the calf of the leg should fall just behind the cinch and remain there all the time you are riding. The stirrup should be short enough so that your knee will be at a sharp

angle and will lie against the shoulder; then you can use the calf of your leg and your knee to exert the pressure that establishes two of the controls. The rider's weight should be distributed equally between the pelvis and the knee with very little weight on the stirrup itself. This will put the bulk of his weight just behind the withers. (Fig. 44)

A good comparison at this time is valuable in order to under-

Fig. 43   Correct stirrup length.

Fig. 44   Rider with weight correctly distributed.

stand why the weight should be placed close to the withers. Soldiers or campers who must carry a pack on their back for any distance soon discover that there is one particular spot where more weight can be carried easier than anywhere else. That spot is directly between the shoulder blades. The pack should be strapped tightly so that it does not flop about uncomfortably. The same condition holds true with a colt; you must be careful to sit in a fixed position so that you do not disturb the colt or throw him off balance. Then, as his muscles develop, he will be better able to handle the additional weight of the rider. With confidence that the rider will remain in a fixed position, the colt will become light and maneuverable quickly.

When you are sure that the colt is passive, pick up the reins and attempt to flex the head with the bridle. You may notice that the colt does not flex as well as when you drove him. The reason for this is that you are carrying the rein from a higher angle, and the colt must have time to adjust himself. Before flexing the head, always raise the reins first so that the bit will slide up to the corners of his mouth. (Fig. 45) When the head has been raised, slack the rein so that the bit will slide back down to the bars of the mouth, and with your hands carried in a lower position, a slight pull will create the flexion desired. You should do this until the colt understands he must keep his head in the position you put it in and not move it until you ask him to.

I would like to stress the fact that a colt should not be guided or reined by his head and neck. All you want of this area is to be able to place it in whatever position you desire, regardless of what the rest of the body is doing. As you approach some of the more intricate exercises in the colt's training, you will understand the principle involved.

When the colt is flexing well from the saddle, you should attempt to bring his head around so that his nose will touch his shoulder from either side, just as you did from the ground in the process of following the hand. (Fig. 46) You should not attempt any more from the saddle

Fig. 45 Achieving desired flexion.

FIG. 46   Establishing control for lessons to follow.

other than being able to mount him. Having the process of following the hand from the saddle well established gives you more control for the lessons to follow and assures you that the colt is definitely in the area of Pattern B.

As you may have noticed, I do not mention how many days, weeks or months it requires to perfect these exercises. You must understand that time is not important—just that you must master each step as you go along. You will know when it has been mastered.

SADDLES

It would be impractical for me to prescribe one particular type of saddle or bridle to be used in the process of schooling the colt as you could have any one of a number of equestrian divisions as your goal, and, of course, you would have to conform to the rules of that division insofar as equipment was concerned.

The only recommendation I can make is to use a saddle that is comfortable and that allows you to adjust your balance as you need to. For instance, some saddles force the rider to sit far down with his legs forward of the cinch. This prevents him from being able to keep his weight over the center of gravity, which is a point approximately four to six inches behind the horse's elbow. Some forward-seat saddles throw the rider's weight too far forward and are just as undesirable. You should try to strike a happy medium, using a saddle that will allow you to distribute your weight as you need it.

BITS

There are numerous bits on the market today. Practically all of them are designed to inflict pain to some degree. If they are used to inflict pain, the schooling of the colt will come to a standstill, and I can assure you that your accomplishments will be very limited. The bit should only be used gently to guide the head and neck and to keep the head flexed in the proper position so that the colt will be able to adjust his own balance. It would be difficult to recommend any specific bit as it should conform with the division in which you are interested.

I will say this. In divisions requiring a curb bit, either alone or with a snaffle, you should examine the colt's mouth and determine what type of curb would fit. Some colts have a very shallow lower jaw. Some also have a thick tongue. If either of these is the case, the port should be wide and high so that the part of the bit which comes in contact with the bars of the colt's mouth can do so without pinching the colt's tongue. However, you must keep the chin strap fairly snug, for if the chin strap or chain is loose, it will cause the high part to rake the roof of the colt's mouth with the slightest pull on the reins; but if you keep the proper tension on the chin strap or chain, this can not happen. Don't use a high port bit unless necessary.

When a colt tosses his head for no apparent reason, it is a sure sign of bit discomfort. Be on the lookout for this, and periodically exam his mouth to see whether any corrective measures should be taken. It would be a good idea to try several types of bits, allowing enough time with each one so that you may find the bit that fits the best. I consider the comfort of the colt's mouth the most important factor in the making of a horse. If the colt's mouth is uncomfortable, too much of his attention will be drawn to this discomfort and the results will be a constant frustration each time he is ridden. Therefore it would be wise for you to pay special attention to his mouth in order to get the best results.

6 / RIDING THE HORSE

MOVING OUT

THE NEXT STEP will be to move the colt forward. (Fig. 47) I would like to stress the fact that while the colt is in motion, you should carry most of your weight between the pelvis and the knee, with a minimum amount of weight on the stirrup. This is most important, as the distribution of weight in the saddle helps control the forequarter and the hindquarter.

Now, sitting in the position just mentioned, with the reins in your left hand—the colt's head flexed slightly—and a short riding whip in your right hand, lay the whip on the colt's croup gently. Then shift your weight from your knees and pelvis to your legs so that most of your weight is now resting on the stirrups. Squeeze both legs and almost simultaneously use the word command, "Come on," while tapping the whip on the croup. As soon as any forward movement is detected, rock back up on your knees and pelvis, lean forward slightly, and continue to squeeze until the colt is walking forward. If the colt should slow down, squeeze again. If the colt should stop, go through the entire procedure previously described. When the colt is walking forward well, do not attempt to turn him. Just walk straight ahead.

THE STOP

It is evident what the next move is. You must teach the colt to stop. Remember to keep your weight close to the colt's withers while he is in motion, with little weight on the stirrups themselves. To pre-

Fig. 47   Moving forward.

pare to stop, raise his head and increase the flexion so that the head and neck are directed toward the rear. Direct your weight back to your feet without standing up in the stirrups, and while squeezing with both legs, give the word command, "Whoa." The colt should stop. The reason for shifting your weight is to assist the colt in shifting his own weight.

When a colt is asked to move forward, you must momentarily transfer the bulk of his weight to his hindquarter so that he will lighten the forehand and be able to move forward. Also, when you ask him to stop, he will attempt to shift his weight toward his hindquarter to lighten his forehand, as his forelegs are not strong enough to take the full impact of both the rider and his own weight at the same time. But when the colt is in motion, you expect him to go balanced, so you sit in a balanced position. You should continue taking all the time needed to move the colt forward and stop him without turning. But do not expect the colt to do a sliding stop at this phase of his training. That will come later.

THE THREE MASTER CONTROLS FROM THE SADDLE

Now that you have the colt so that you can mount him, flex his head and neck, move him out, and stop him as directed, the next step is apparent. You must teach him to turn from the saddle. *You should never allow the colt to turn to the pull of the rein.* Instead, he must turn away from the pressure against his shoulder. I am sure you now realize that these movements are simply a repetition of what we did from the ground, and in exactly the same order. If you can understand the principles so far, you will go a long way with your efforts.

Just as you considered the colt as being in three sections when you started to work him from the ground, you should do the same from the saddle. You have already mastered the following of the hand with the bridle, so you now go to the second part of the colt: the control of the hindquarter or the pivot on the forehand.

Sit in the saddle in a balanced position with more weight on your knees and pelvis than on the stirrups. With the rein in the right hand, you flex the colt a little. Before executing a movement, always flex the head a little to prepare the colt for what is to come. In your left hand carry a riding whip. Place your left hand along the colt's left side just behind the calf of your left leg. Still holding the whip, drop your weight back down to the stirrups on both legs. This will put the colt in the standard position to execute a command. Now drop the bulk of your weight on the right stirrup. This will throw the colt's weight to his left hind leg as that is the leg that is preparing to drive him over. Now with a pressure of your left leg coming from below the knee, the colt should move over with the assistance of your left hand. (Fig. 48) If the colt does not move, a quick tap with the whip on the colt's flanks will move him over while your right hand on the rein steadies his head.

When you wish to stop the movement, drop your weight on both stirrups, being careful not to lean forward or the colt will move forward, then rock up to a balanced position again. This exercise should be done on both sides until the colt will readily move away from the pressure of the leg. Be sure to make only one complete pivot on the foreleg. Do it on both sides. Only after this has been mastered, should you attempt to go further. In the meantime you should constantly review past achievements, going progressively forward. It will be well worth it as the colt you are training could become a schooled horse of Olympic calibre if you follow these instructions faithfully.

After control of the hindquarters has been mastered, you should begin to school the colt on the third control—the control of the forequarters. At this point I do not say, as many authors do, "This will be difficult," "You must have patience," "You must keep trying." I maintain that the next control should be quite simple, as you have schooled your colt thoroughly and with a purpose, while always preparing for the exercises to come.

Sit in a balanced position, with the rein in your left hand. Flex a little. With the whip in your right hand, put your hand against the colt's right shoulder. Now bring the colt's head slightly to the right. Drop your weight down on both stirrups to the preparatory position

FIG. 48   Control of the forequarters from the saddle.

you will always use. Now drop your weight to your right leg and right knee equally. With knee and thigh, create a pressure against the right shoulder of the colt. If the colt does not then move away, a quick tap of the whip on the right shoulder should accomplish it. Your left hand keeps the head always a little right of center to prevent the colt's hindquarters from moving to the right. Soon he should be walking around himself doing a pivot on his hindquarters. (Fig. 49) You should practice this on both sides.

The quicker the pressure, the faster he should move. Do not attempt to do a wheelabout or a rollback in the air as the colt is not ready for that yet. That will come later. When the colt has mastered the control of the forequarter so that he moves away from the pressure of the knee and thigh, you should be able to turn him whether he is moving or standing still.

STOP AND TURN AT A WALK

We will proceed much the same as we did from the ground. Move the colt forward, stop, pivot on the hind leg a half turn, and walk back in the direction from which you came; stop, turn again on the opposite side. The colt will begin to enjoy this if you do not overdo it. If you wish to turn the colt gently without pivoting, simply apply pressure to the shoulder without coming to a stop. This should result in a gradual turn while in motion.

All the turning so far has been done without the use of the bit, and you should continue with this principle throughout the colt's training. *Review all these exercises each day at the walk only.* Do not attempt to trot or canter until you are ready for it. Until now, the colt has not been ready for it. You will see why after you have completed the next exercise.

FIG. 49   Control of the hindquarters from the saddle.

The Three Enforcers

Go back to the exercises used for extension and collection. By this time, when you give the command, "Under," the colt ought to put his legs far under his body. Before attempting to execute the same maneuver from the saddle, however, you need to be better acquainted with the principles involved.

You should understand thoroughly the three controls you have learned about, as these three controls, if they are perfected, are all you need to create any movement in horsemanship. In order to reach perfection, you must establish the fact that with the three controls, you have three enforcers to back them up. The enforcer for the first control, that of the head and neck, is of course the bit. The enforcer for the second control, that of the hindquarters, is the spur. The enforcer for the third control, the control of the forequarters, is the whip. Three controls, three enforcers. The bit should be used to guide and reprimand, if necessary—the spur and the whip also, but only in the areas they enforce.

Once you put on the spur, never use the whip behind the cinch, only on the shoulder after the gaits have been mastered.

The Lesson of the Spur

You should now select a pair of spurs. Regardless of what type of horse you intend to finish with, whether it be a reining horse, hunter, pleasure, dressage, or polo pony, you should start with the same type of spur. It should be of either Spanish or Western design, with at least a two-inch or larger rowel. The rowel should be dull with no sharp points or edges. This design will have a definite reaction, the kind you want to establish.

Sit on the colt in a balanced position, the rein in your left hand. Raise the colt's head as high as possible, still having it flexed. Hold the rein firmly with your fingers. Do not pull, just hold, as the reaction you are about to get is apt to cause the colt to lower his head, and he will do this by pulling the rein through your fingers. So be prepared to see that this does not happen. The whip should be in your right hand and held just over the croup. Now drop your weight to the stirrups without standing up, and simultaneously squeeze your legs so that the broad sides of the spurs come against the colt's side. At the same time say, "Under," with a quick tap on the croup. If you do not feel the colt's legs shoot under, you will need to do this more forcefully. First, rock back up to a balanced position and proceed exactly as before, only now when the word command, "Under," is given, turn your toes out so that the points of the dull rowels come against the colt's side. Now raise both feet while keeping pressure on the spur so that the rowel will roll two or three inches up on the colt's side. Immediately, the colt will react strongly in Pattern A behavior. He may even try to buck. If you hold his head up, you can prevent a buck.

Rock back up to a balanced position and caress the colt to return him to the behavior of Pattern B. This is a part of the instruction I give with reluctance, as, throughout, I have stressed the fact of not exciting the colt. Now I am telling you to make it happen deliberately. However, there is a reason for this. Just as the bit and the whip were introduced so that the colt would respect but not fear them, you must also accomplish this with the spur. You may never have to do it again if the impression on the colt has been strong enough. The pinching, rolling action was an experience he is not likely to forget.

You should continue this exercise until the colt shoots his legs well under. Be careful only to use the pressure of the calf of the leg at first, and gradually, if the colt does not become excited, bring the broad side of the rowel against the colt's side. This should be practiced also at a walk, stop, and turn—both ways.

You should be getting the feel of fine horsemanship, as by now the colt should be well balanced, stopping and turning on his hindquarters. *Do not overdo it.* Execute only four or five stops and turns a day as the colt is still not well muscled.

GETTING ACQUAINTED WITH NEW OBJECTS, PLACES AND CONDITIONS

From the time of his birth, the colt should constantly be introduced to new objects and conditions; lead him through water and

over wooden planks, and allow him to go close to automobiles, machinery, trailers, etc., so that he will gradually accept them without fear.

A horse is a routinist, and if he is not hurt in any way, he will accept the object as being friendly and harmless. However, if anything should hurt him, it will be very difficult for him to accept it later in his training. Shying is a condition expected with most young horses, and the rider should be on his guard constantly to prevent an upset. As the horse develops mentally, his tendency to shy will decrease. (Figs. 50, 51)

FIGS. 50, 51   Getting acquainted with places, objects, and conditions.

7 / TWO TRACKING

HOW TO EXECUTE THE SIDE PASS

THE SIDE PASS is a combination of the use of the second and third controls on the same side simultaneously. The purpose of this exercise is to develop muscles that do not ordinarily become developed through regular riding. It is also an important control for the change of leads at the canter.

You commence this exercise by sitting in a balanced position, holding the rein in your left hand, the whip in your right. Drop your weight to the stirrups to collect the colt behind; raise the rein, flex, and collect the colt in front. Now, drop your weight to the colt's right side equally between the thigh and lower leg. Create a pressure with the lower part of your leg as though pivoting on the forehand one step. Transfer the pressure to the thigh and knee so that the forequarter will take one step to the left. Continue alternating the pressure from your calf to your thigh and knee.

The colt should be moving sideways in a rocking motion. Soon you should merge the pressure of the thigh, knee, and calf simultaneously. This, with practice, will produce the true side pass. (Fig. 52) Do this on both sides often until you have mastered it. Meanwhile, brush up on past achievements as well. Be sure to guide the colt with the balance of the head and neck. Use the whip and spur to enforce control of the quarters if necessary. But remember, if the spur is misused the colt will not move away from it, but will move into it instead.

FIG. 52   The true side pass.

LATERAL FLEXIONS

After the colt is working well at the side pass, you should go to another exercise. It is commonly called the half pass or a form of two-tracking. (Fig. 53) While the colt is doing a side pass, lean forward, at the same time bringing the pressure of the leg that has been passive back into play, but still keep your weight in the same place so that you will not lose the motion sideways. Now, you are going forward and sideways at the same time.

After you are going well with this exercise, commence new flexion that will carry the colt's head almost to the shoulder without changing the direction you are going in. This should not be difficult, as the colt has been taught not to move his body when you move his head and neck.

Another exercise that can help create the suppleness so necessary to allow the horse to perform with ease is the "shoulders fore." (Fig. 54) This exercise is started while walking straight ahead. Gently bring the head and neck to one side, causing the shoulder of the horse to be leading. There are several combinations of this movement known as "shoulders in" and "quarters in." (Fig. 55) All can be done in a left or right position. The terminology is not of great importance, but the movements are. They are simply a combination of the aids with which you are familiar, done in motion, namely, the control and yielding of the forequarters, hindquarters, and the head. Bringing these controls into play in varying degrees should be practiced often. The new flexions will develop and make supple the many muscles needed to produce the unity you are striving for.

After this exercise has been mastered, you have the necessary reaction established to produce the trot, canter, and change of leads.

Fig. 53   The half-pass.

Fig. 54 Shoulders fore.

Fig. 55 Shoulders in.

8 / THE WALK

Aｌｔｈｏｕｇｈ ｙｏｕ ｈａｖｅ ａｌｒｅａｄｙ been riding the horse at a walk, some consideration should now be given to refinement in the walk. It has been my experience that if all the variations of the walk have been mastered, the horse will be able to do well in other gaits including their many variations.

To begin with, the walk is a four-beat movement starting with the left fore as No. 1, the right fore as No. 2, the left hind as No. 3, and the right hind as No. 4. If the horse does not pick his hind feet up in the sequence just mentioned, the gait he is doing cannot be a walk.

There are several mongrel gaits, sometimes created by man, sometimes resulting from injury to the horse. One of these peculiar gaits is when the horse canters behind while walking in front, or vice versa. These off gaits, if I may call them such, in some cases are very comfortable to ride and do not seem to cause any great discomfort to the horse, but they are not included as any part of the three natural gaits normally used.

The relaxed, or free walk, of course, is very simple, and the horse will perform this without any assistance from his rider provided you give him a free rein. The collected walk is quite different. (Fig. 56) The horse must carry his head and neck in a balanced position. The movement must have considerable cadence as well as impulsion. The

96

FIG. 56 Collected walk.

rider must be careful to increase impulsion without increasing speed. The horse must accept impulsion without going behind the bit.

In the extended walk the rider should extend his hands forward allowing the horse to stretch his head and neck forward, still maintaining some contact on the bit. (Fig. 57) This movement also requires a fair amount of impulsion, and the horse will move forward with a cadenced swing. The extended walk is a variation of the relaxed walk. If speeded up without the horse breaking his gait, the four-beat cadence of the walk will disappear and the two-beat cadence of the pace will take over, and the footfalls will be left fore and left hind together, and right fore and right hind together. Also, in the pace there is a point of suspension when all four legs are off the ground.

The speeding up of the collected walk will create still another type of walk which is called the rack. While at the collected walk, if the horse is pushed forward while still maintaining the same cadence and is not allowed to stretch his head and neck forward, thus having his reach restricted, he will be moving in the very pronounced four-beat cadence of the rack. It is not necessary to school the pace and rack as they are only terminations of the collected and extended walk, but if your aims are directed toward this division of the sport, you have some idea of how they are created.

Fig. 57 Extended walk.

9 / THE TROT

You should first attempt to create the trot from a standstill. The trot is a diagonal gait, which means that the left forefoot and the right hind foot work together. The right forefoot and the left hind foot work together also. (Fig. 58) Both forelegs and both hind legs work in opposition to each other. In other words, in the trot, two forelegs or two hind legs cannot be on the ground at the same time. The impulsion to create the trot comes from the hindquarter. By taking advantage of this knowledge, plus the controls you have mastered, it is fairly simple to create the trot from a standstill.

The reason I stress that the trot must be started from a standstill is because the colt must be taught to stay in the gait you put him in until asked to stop.

This way you will have less trouble when training for a fast walk or a fast trot. There will be less chance of the colt's breaking gait.

You should start this exercise sitting in a balanced position, carrying the whip in your right hand with both hands on the rein. Raise the head as high as possible, still flexed, and drop your weight to collect. Now, drop your weight to the left side, using the leg strongly. Then to the right side using it strongly. This causes the colt to shift his weight from one side to the other, creating the trot. Then lift the head and neck upward and forward, lean forward strongly, and give the command, "Come on."

100

Figs. 58, 59, 60   Collected trot.

The instant forward motion is indicated, drop your weight to both stirrups, squeezing strongly, and rock up to a balanced position while still using your legs to create the impulsion necessary to produce a good trot. Begin to post off the knees, keeping the lower part of the leg as still as possible. Within a few weeks you will be doing a good strong trot, if you keep your hands light on the bit and don't try to hang on by the use of the rein.

You may notice that, while the colt flexed well at the walk, he is not doing as well now. This is due to the faster movement. If you take it slowly and worry his head back down, in time you will again have the flexion desired. If you trot three times to the right, go three times to the left, so that the colt will develop evenly on both sides.

After the aids for the trot have been well established, we can begin to think about improving it and schooling for variations of the trot. As I stated before, the trot is a diagonal gait and will remain such; otherwise it ceases to be a trot.

Before we can proceed with improving the trot, there is much we should know and understand. The horse, natural, without a rider, is perfectly capable of regulating his speed, impulsion, extension, or collection as he wishes, but once bridled and saddled, his natural way of going disappears in most cases. There are *some* horses that remain supple and natural and require little training. However, we are more concerned with the horse that requires guidance from his handler, and with regard to this horse, the quality of his trot will depend entirely on how the aids are applied.

To most people, even some professional trainers, it is very difficult to analyze exactly what creates good trotting action. The basis for a good trot is that the horse must be supple and at ease with his rider. This is of paramount importance. He should flex well and accept leg pressure without becoming excited. The horse should feel as natural as possible, as only with this feeling of ease will he have the suppleness to function as nature intended. If he cannot feel at ease, he will produce a peculiar, uneven, frustrated sort of trot. This frustrated trot is quite common at many of our horse shows today, and there are some people who mistake the frustrated action for a brilliant trot even though there may be absolutely no cadence present. A horse becomes excited when asked to do this kind of a trot for a very good reason.

While standing still, a horse's weight is distributed equally: half is supported through his hind legs and the other half through his forelegs with the center of gravity being an imaginary point between his hind legs and his forelegs. This point is commonly accepted as being four to six inches behind the elbow of the foreleg, perpendicular to the ground, or just behind the cinch. The center of gravity can vary according to the conformation of the horse.

If the horse has good conformation and is well balanced, the center of gravity should be as previously described. The minute the horse is in motion, the weight of his forequarters and hindquarters will be directed toward the center of gravity. The reason for this is quite obvious. The horse can only see where he places his forelegs. Never can a horse see where his hindlegs will tread. However, nature has taken care of him so that he won't step in or on anything that would injure him in any way by allowing his hind leg to be placed exactly where his foreleg has just left. (Fig. 59) This insures the horse's safety. The horse can only do this with a rider on him if he feels at ease and is balanced.

Once we have the horse trotting balanced, with his hind legs placed exactly where the forelegs have just left, we have established the nucleus of a good trot. Even though the horse may place his hind legs where they should be, he may lack impulsion. Impulsion is simply the lowering of the hocks, so that when he starts the drive with either hind leg, it will propel his body upward and forward creating a point of suspension where all four feet are off the ground. At this point he will shift his weight to the other diagonal and will alternate diagonals while he is air-borne.

If the horse lacks impulsion, he cannot become air-borne. The result will be considerable weight thrown on the foreleg because it strikes the ground short of its original reach. This action is commonly called "dwelling action" or "flyswatting."

In the proper three-gaited trot, while one diagonal assumes a high degree of collection, the other diagonal assumes a high degree of extension. (Fig. 60) With his neck curved in a beautiful arch, the drive is started with the horse's hind leg well under his body, the hock low to the ground. With a lifting, driving motion, the horse is propelled upward and forward with the drive terminating far behind the point of vertical. This will cause the horse to have all four feet off

Fig. 59

the ground. He'll glide through the air with a floating motion, only to land with the hind leg of the other diagonal far under the body and the hock low to the ground; the front leg, in sympathy with this diagonal, will strike the ground slightly after. (Fig. 61) Then the same cycle is repeated over and over with each diagonal. Needless to say the height and length of the float, accompanied by good rhythm and head carriage, determines the brilliance of the trot. This trot is taught without the use of weights or any mechanical apparatus.

The extended trot is the same as the trot I have just described except that the head and neck of the horse are allowed to be extended forward causing the horse to travel in a long form. This trot, of course, is not as brilliant as the collected version, although it contains all the basic properties. As in the collected trot, there is a moment of suspension, although it is hardly visible, because the extension of the head

FIG. 60

and neck places more weight on the forequarters, preventing the horse from being as high off the ground as he was in the collected trot. Also, the hind leg should tread exactly on the spot where the foreleg has just left. The speed of the extended trot can vary from a very slow jog trot to a very fast trot, but the head and neck must be extended forward with a slight contact on the bit.

The passage, or the elevated trot, and the piaffer, or "trot in place," as seen in the dressage arena, are simply slowed down variations of the collected or three-gaited trot. (Fig. 62) The slower the

Fɪɢ. 61   Three-gaited trot.

horse moves forward, the greater the impulsion needed. The point of suspension becomes so marked that the horse seems to be going in slow motion.

So you can see that the horse has only one kind of trot, with its variations, which are simply collection and extension at varying speeds from the piaffer to the very fast trot seen at harness races. The rider can find the correct way to create these variations of the trot as he progresses, using the aids with which he is already familiar and constantly being aware of the fact that the horse must remain quiet and supple.

Fig. 62 The passage.

10 / REIN BACK

I HAVE WITHHELD DISCUSSING this movement, as the rein back is comparatively easy, and it hasn't been necessary to execute it from the saddle. The complex mental behavior of the colt is not too hard to understand. If the colt, working well in the area of Pattern B, is asked to execute a new exercise that may be rather difficult for him to grasp, he will immediately try to please us by performing another movement that he has mastered, and usually this movement will be the rein back. So, by not introducing the rein back sooner, we have not been plagued with this overanticipation on the colt's part. Going further into an analysis of the rein back, I have found that, contrary to the belief of most trainers, a colt uses the impulsion of his forelegs to propel him backwards—not his hindquarters. Many trainers claim that the aids used for the rein back are the same as the aids used to stop. This is not true. In the stop most of the colt's weight is on the forequarters. As you already know, in order to execute any movement, you must put your weight close to the point of impulsion. This is also true when backing up.

Start the exercise sitting in a balanced position, holding the rein in your left hand and the whip in your right hand. Drop your weight to the stirrups, collecting the colt, flexing the head at the same time. As the impulsion needed to back the colt must come from the front legs, you should place the bulk of your weight on the knees and thighs. Lean backward slightly to indicate the direction you wish to go in, and lower his head. Then, with a tremorlike action on the bit, and short jerks, use the word command, "Back up," at the same time. If the colt is not backing up by now, a sharp tap, first on one shoulder then on the other, with the whip should increase impulsion on both front legs alternately, and the colt will back up. You must, of course, create pressure with your knee and thigh at the same time. As soon as the colt is moving backwards release the pressure, remaining balanced. When you wish to stop, drop your weight on both stirrups and squeeze with pressure coming from the calves of your legs. Soon the colt will back up on leg pressure alone, and you should use the bit only for balancing purposes.

11 / THE CANTER

THE COLT'S ACTION in the canter is much different from the diagonal movements of the trot. In the canter, both front legs and hind legs work together, or nearly so. (Fig. 63) The canter is started off the hindquarters with both legs under the body. The colt lifts his forequarters in the air, then drives upward and forward with his hindquarters. There is a moment of suspension when all four feet are in the air, then the front legs strike the ground in a rolling motion and the colt comes to rest again on his hindquarters. This, repeated over and over slowly, causes the undulating movement of the canter.

However, there are other things you should understand before starting the canter. To begin with, horses, like people, are usually right handed; and horses, like people, feel more secure when they do things with their right hand, particularly under pressure. To analyze further: some authors have gone so far as to say that all horses are left handed, because, when you start off into a canter, invariably the horse will start on a left lead. Part of this is true. Most horses prefer to start on a left lead while still untrained, because of the fact that they are right handed. It is the right hind leg of the horse which does the driving when a horse is in the left lead, and the left hind leg does the most work when you are in a right lead. The lead side simply indicates the direction you turn into and acts as a balance when you turn. Also, when a horse starts into a left lead, he must step slightly to his

FIG. 63　The canter

left starting the canter, and going into a right lead, he must step slightly to his right side.

It must be understood that the canter is a relatively faster movement than the walk or trot; that is, in its basic form. With the increase of speed comes the increase of excitement, and, of course, with excitement the horse will revert to Pattern A. So, much tact must be used to return his behavior gently to Pattern B. The best way to accomplish this is to canter him only a short distance, about thirty or forty feet, return to a walk on a loose rein, caress him to show your appreciation, then canter him again and return to a walk. This procedure will not only teach the horse to be relaxed at the canter, but also his starts and stops will become much better because this exercise gives you the opportunity to practice the transitions more often.

When the canter has been worked down to a point where a reasonably active motion is present and flexion has returned to normal, you should start to think about the variations of the canter. The same conditions are true with the canter that you observed at the trot relative to where the horse places his hind legs. Of course, in order to prevent injury to himself, he must place his hind legs in exactly the same spot his forelegs have just left, and the horse will do so only if he is supple and calm.

With this information in mind, you should start the colt from a standstill into a canter on the left lead.

Sit in a balanced position with rein in your left hand and whip in your right. Have the whip in position close to the colt's right hindquarter. Drop your weight and collect, then drop your weight to the right stirrup, lift the head upward and slightly to the right. This will help lighten the left side. Tap the colt on his right hindquarter several times, while using pressure from your left leg. When forward motion is detected, rock back to a balanced position, using your legs strongly. If the movement diminishes into a trot, use the whip again. Soon the colt will be galloping with hardly any flexion of the head and neck visible, because of the faster motion. Caress him while in motion by stroking his neck. Gradually bring his head lower, sit straighter in the saddle, and encourage him to slow down a little.

There are only two variations of the canter. Number one is the long form or the extended canter. (Fig. 64) In this form the head and neck of the horse are allowed to stretch forward placing more weight on the forequarter. This restricts the moment of suspension so that the horse is not air-borne quite as high as he would be in the collected form. The speed can vary from a very slow lope, usually seen in Western classes, to a very fast gallop characteristic of a race horse. The speed should be regulated by the lean of your body, not

FIGS. 64, 65   The extended canter.

by tugging on the rein. The slower the movement, the straighter you sit, the greater the lean, the faster you will go. (Fig. 65) There is very little head flexion visible at the extended canter and only a slight contact with the bit to help the horse understand he must slow down or speed up with the lean of your body. You can use the rein together with your change of lean at first and use an increase of leg pressure to speed up. Soon by only using the weight of your body, you can make the horse speed up and slow down. Practice this often until you have perfected it.

Number two is the short form or the collected canter. (Fig. 66) This is the variation used in dressage or three-gaited classes. It is much different from the extended form as the head and neck are carried much higher with good flexion of the head and with the hocks

FIG. 65

lower to the ground with greater impulsion. The point of suspension is definitely visible, and the undulations have a positive rhythm. The speed of this canter varies from cantering on the spot to the very fast hand gallop. The variation of speed can be schooled in the same manner used in the extended canter. The slower you go, the greater the impulsion. You must teach the horse to increase impulsion without increasing the speed, as you apply the leg aids. He should only increase speed with the lean or distribution of your weight. Constantly increase speed, slow down, increase impulsion, then increase speed. Do this over and over, but stop frequently to praise your horse.

If your aims are focused at dressage competitions, you should work to a point where the horse will do three or four undulations at the canter on the spot. This will put you in a good position to school

Fig. 66   The collected canter.

the pirouettes at the canter when the time comes. A very slow, schooled canter will make it much easier to teach the change of leads at short intervals, and of course these changes are mandatory in dressage competitions. The pirouette at the canter is very similar to the turn on the haunches that you have already mastered. The difference between the two is the position of the hind legs. In the turn on the haunches, the horse holds one hind leg anchored as he walks around it. In the pirouette, the horse must keep cantering all the time. (Fig. 67) While his forequarters move around his hindquarters, his hindquarters must keep cantering up and down without losing cadence.

Many trainers have great difficulty in schooling this movement because they rely too much on slowing the horse through the bridle. Consequently, the horse loses impulsion, and the movement ceases to be a canter. Keep this in mind, and use the bridle as little as possible. You will have far more satisfactory results.

The rest will be up to your own discretion, as by now you can honestly say you know something about schooling horses. Just as you wish the colt to work quietly with suppleness and without excitement, you must also assume the same attitude toward yourself. Make sure that you do not stiffen and that you always remain in a balanced position regardless of the gait or speed. Always lean in the direction in which you are going. After the colt has started his movement, the faster the speed, the greater the lean. Always carry your arms in such a position that there is a straight line between your forehand and rein to the bit, regardless of the lean.

I realize that the descriptions of starting the trot and canter may sound a little difficult and complicated. Actually, I have tried to give a detailed, slow-motion description, so to speak. Each movement is a momentary part of a whole, and the movements should flow smoothly. Once you have started the trot and canter this way, you will understand readily what I mean.

FIG. 67   The pirouette at the canter.

12 / THE LEADS

The Canter on the Right Lead

This movement should be executed in the same manner used to start the canter on the left lead. (Fig. 68) Much precaution must be taken that you do not stiffen in the saddle. Remain calm and relaxed. This will help the colt feel the same way. Do not shout or use the spur. Be sure to bring the fore and hindquarters to the right simultaneously. If you use the spur, the colt will push into it causing his hindquarters to move to the left, and he will remain on the left lead behind, even though he is on a right lead in front. This most undesirable action is called a crosslead.

It is not only uncomfortable to ride, but very dangerous. It puts the fore and hind leg on the left side of the colt too close together, making it possible for his left hind leg to grab his left fore. The result could be a bad fall and a possible broken leg for the colt, not to mention what might happen to the rider.

I repeat—*Do not use the spur!*

If the colt will not do the canter on the right lead the first time, go back and review the control of the quarters until you have really mastered them. After you have mastered the start on the right lead, exercise the colt at both the trot and canter and in the halfpass, increasing flexions accordingly. If good flexion is evident and the colt goes well at the halfpass both ways, you are now ready for the flying change of leads or the change of leads in the air.

118

Fɪɢ. 68   Canter on the left lead.

SIMPLE CHANGE OF LEAD

After the starts at the canter have been mastered on both the left
and right lead, you should practice the simple change of lead. This
is best accomplished cantering on a straight line. *Do not practice this
movement at the figure eight.* As a matter of fact, to practice the
simple or flying change of leads through a figure eight would do much
more harm than good. I do not recommend. it. I will explain it in
more detail with the instructions of the flying change of leads. Now
back again to the simple change of leads. You should canter straight
about thirty or forty feet, make a smooth transition to the walk, then
walk about ten to twelve steps and again start cantering on the opposite lead from the one on which you had previously been cantering.
This will acquaint the horse with the aids being used alternately and
will help you considerably with the flying change of leads. (Fig. 69)

COUNTER LEAD

The counter lead is one of the many exercises that should be
perfected in order to establish a fluent, positive response from the
horse when he is asked, through the aids, to yield or hold—whatever
the case may be. Before you are ready to execute the counter lead,
the horse should be an expert at cantering small circles. You should
start on a circle about fifty feet in diameter and gradually work down
until you are cantering a circle of about twenty-five feet in diameter.
Gently bring the head and neck over so that the horse's spine forms
a crescent with the circle, that is to say, the horse is bent from his poll
to his tail. These new flexions will become very important in regard
to other movements that will be explained later. Practice one circle

Fig. 69   Canter on a counter lead.

going to the left on a left lead and to the right on a right lead. When good flexion of the spine is evident, you should be ready for the counter lead.

You start the exercise through a serpentine which is nothing more than a series of half circles about fifty feet in diameter connected together in a straight line, and of course each half circle would be in reverse of the one before it. Start cantering the first half circle on a left lead. As you approach the end of the half circle, gently apply your left knee and thigh to the horse's shoulder. Bring the head and neck to the right still maintaining enough pressure with your right leg (and this pressure should come from below the knee), so that you can prevent the horse from changing leads. That is precisely the object of this lesson.

Most horses are taught to change leads when the rider changes direction. A well-schooled horse only changes leads when his rider asks him to.

So as you proceed cantering the serpentine, you will be on the correct lead half of the time and on a counter lead the other half. Make sure that the horse is flexed properly. At first he will try to go sideways somewhat rather than flex his spine while he is on the counter lead. If you take it slow and do not excite the horse, he will settle down and execute the counter lead fairly well. Even in its best form, the counter lead is rather awkward but necessary.

FLYING CHANGE OF LEADS

The flying change of leads is exactly what the title implies. It is done at the point of suspension while the horse has all four feet off the ground and without interrupting the undulation of the canter. The flying change should be executed in a straight line, and the horse should be straight from his poll to his tail.

Many books and instructions for beginners make the grave mistake in teaching the change of leads through the figure eight, and the result, in most cases, is disastrous.

In regard to further schooling of the change of leads, I will try to explain the reason it is not practical. In the first place, the figure eight comprises two small circles joined together, not two teardrops longer than they are wide. Let's assume that the horse is cantering to the left on a small circle. As he completes the circle and approaches the point where the other circle joins, the horse will be flexed to his left in contour with the circle he is cantering on. Now if a change of leads were asked for at that point, the horse would have to straighten and bend to conform with the circle to the right and change leads at the same time. The rider also would have his problems trying to apply all the aids properly, which of course would excite the horse, and a correct change would be very difficult to execute.

The change of leads at the figure eight as just described *is* the correct way but only by a horse and rider who have mastered the change of leads on a straightaway first. By learning on the straightaway you do not have the problem of unbending and reflexing as you would on the circle. Many riders, supposedly changing leads through a figure eight, upon completing the first circle to the left, turn their horse sharply to the left and then sharply to the right, and sometimes they manage to come out of it on a right lead. But the horse has only learned to change leads when the rider changes direction, and this is of little value as far as horsemanship is concerned.

I would like to explain why a horse should never be taught to change leads when you change direction. In the game of polo or stock horse reining patterns, pole bending, barrel racing, etc., the time element is very important and a fraction of a second could mean a lot. So we should prepare the horse so that he will not be handicapped in any way as far as lost time is concerned. Yet many riders in the fields just mentioned school their horses to change leads when the rider changes direction, losing valuable seconds and endangering the safety of both horse and rider.

I have observed and clocked the change of leads many times on the straightaway and on the curve, and I find that a horse will slow down when asked to change while he is turning and will speed up when asked to change on the straightaway. Also it is asking too much for the horse to change and turn at the same time. Often the horse will fall down when asked to do this. If the change is made even one step before you turn, the horse can do it correctly and gain time.

A few exercises are necessary before you can execute the flying change of leads, one being the half pass at the canter both ways. (Fig. 70) Another good exercise is the pivot on the haunches, only one step in either direction. This helps to get more accuracy by controlling the forehand through the thigh and knee. Also, the pivot on the forehand, one step in either direction, helps get more control of the haunches through the calf and ankle.

After you have practiced these exercises and feel confident that the horse will yield when you ask him to, you will proceed to execute the flying change of leads in the following manner.

Start the horse cantering on a right lead. The canter should be slow and well cadenced with good flexion of the head and neck. You should be sitting in a relaxed position, back straight, and your legs in slight contact with the horse's body. Your left leg is creating a pressure just a little greater than your right leg so that the horse will know he is doing what you ask of him. You will notice as you canter that the horse's shoulder, neck, and head seem to rise and fall as he completes each cycle of undulation. You should acquaint yourself with the feel of his rising and falling.

There is only one point during the cycle of each undulation when the horse is capable of changing leads, and that point occurs when all four legs are in the air or at the point of suspension. It would be impossible for you to apply aids while he is suspended and

FIG. 70   The half pass at the canter.

have him acknowledge them in time to execute the change, so you should apply the aids for the change just before the horse becomes air-borne. From the saddle the right time can be determined when the horse has reached his lowest point of the undulation. By the time the horse acknowledges the aid, he is just preparing to become air-borne, and the change will not be bungled. The aids for the change of leads are the same as those used to start the canter. Also they are identical to the aids used at the halfpass while cantering.

When you have mastered the flying change of leads, you should begin to school him to change leads at short intervals. This is best accomplished by counting the undulations between changes.

Start cantering on a right lead. Count the undulations to ten, and then make the change to the left side, and count ten more undulations. Gradually work down to five. You should not proceed with the changes at shorter intervals until you have mastered the change at every five intervals. These changes require a great deal of cadence on both sides, from the rider as well as the horse, especially as you approach every other stride, and finally, one of the hardest movements of horsemanship, the change of leads every stride.

I have rarely seen this movement, that is, the change of lead every stride, executed properly. Some riders, said to be changing leads every stride, really think they are, but if you look closely, you will see that the horse is only changing his forelegs while he remains on the same lead behind. If he remains on the same lead behind, he is on the correct lead half the time and on a cross lead the other half.

This sort of exhibition is worthless. Usually the forelegs go through a spectacular action which appears to be a Spanish Walk at the canter. You will also notice that the rider has all he can do to keep his seat. The violent action of the cross lead is responsible for part of it. The rest lies in the resentment of the horse as he flings himself through this ridiculous movement just to get it over with. Actually, the change of leads every stride, if done properly, is very easy to ride.

It has all the rhythm, suppleness, and cadence of a ballet dance and is one of the requirements of the Grand Prix tests of the Olympic Games. A great fault which can develop is that the horse sometimes becomes so proud of this accomplishment that he will continue to change of his own accord without the aids of the rider. F.E.I.* rules have prevented this from happening at international competitions by requiring a given number of changes, that being fifteen consecutive changes, no more, no less, so that the rider has to govern the exact number in order to execute this movement correctly.

If you have been following instructions carefully and have taken the time to master each exercise as you progressed, the colt will do the change of leads the first time you try. If he does, you really have a colt that is supple, and the possibilities of going further are evident. However, you must bide your time. Do not let this accomplishment drive you forward too quickly. Remember, it takes seven years or longer before the colt is physically and mentally developed. This precaution allows you to have a good working mount for many years to come. Haste makes waste!

*Federation Equestre Internationale. This organization, with headquarters in Brussels, Belgium, is composed of representatives from countries all over the world. The governing board for Olympic equestrian events, it establishes the rules and supplies judges for international equestrian competitions.

13 / FAST STOP

AFTER YOU HAVE MASTERED the change of leads and the colt is going well in a slow canter, with good flexion of the head and body, you can attempt the quick stop. I do not like to use the expression "sliding stop," as too many people get the wrong impression of this movement. Many exclaim how far the horse can slide, forgetting entirely that the purpose of this movement is to stop as quickly as possible without discomfort to either the horse or rider. (Fig. 71) Also, it is important to stop in a balanced position so that if a quick turn is expected, the horse can execute it without delay.

First, let us realize exactly what goes on prior to the stop. In the description of the three types of conformation, I referred to the ideal straight-legged horse that can deliver a great deal of extension as well as collection. This type of horse must be helped considerably at the quick stop. Although he may deliver a beautiful, easy canter, it is done with long strides, with the drive beginning far under the body and terminating far behind vertical. If you use the same system of stopping as at the walk, you could run into trouble. If you asked the colt to stop while his hind legs were completing the drive, they would be in the wrong position for him to stop properly. The results would be a series of short jumps with the colt's weight on his forehand. You would have to hang on to keep from sliding up on his neck.

So proceed to canter slowly, acquainting yourself with the rock-

Figs. 71, 72, 73, 74   The fast stop.

ing motion, while watching the lead foot as it strikes the ground. Soon you time yourself to this rhythm. You should ask the colt to stop when the lead foot strikes the ground (Fig. 72), as the hind legs already have started their cycle back under the colt. (Fig. 73) Use the same system to stop as was used at the walk—lifting the head a little higher without pulling on the rein. This will cause him to clear the ground with his front feet when the stop is made. Soon the colt will get used to short distance running and stopping and will shorten his stride making the stop even better.

I might add that a standing-under type of horse would be a little easier to train in this movement. But if the straight-legged horse is trained as prescribed, he will do it better as he has better balance. The standing-under type throws his legs too far forward, causing him to lose his balance temporarily and not recover it quickly enough to do a balanced rollback. You will notice that the standing-under type will slide much farther because of the angle of his legs. He has to throw his weight forward to help balance himself, and consequently, his front legs will strike the ground alternately as though he were still running with his hind legs locked under him. This may be very spectacular to some people, but it's not practical. The standing-over or straight-legged horse will put his legs under, but not too far, using his hocks, stifle, and hips to cushion the stop, keeping his front legs off the ground until the stop has been completed.

After the foundation for the fast stop has been well established, you should acquaint yourself with the many different kinds of stops in the numerous divisions and subdivisions of the sport; but bear in mind that in order for the stop to be correct in any division, the conditions of the previous recommendation *must* be in force, and these are: *the horse should stop as quickly as possible without discomfort to himself or his rider.* Also he should stop in a position where his balance will allow him to make a fast turn if necessary.

FIG. 72

This recommendation applies to almost all divisions of the sport except the roping horse. The stop made by the roping horse is quite different in that its aim is to stop quickly and hold. In order to execute this stop, the horse prepares himself in a crouched position, belly low to the ground, selecting his own balance to brace himself for the tremendous impact about to take place involving three hundred to a thousand pounds of furious bovine. Also he must stop in a position so that he can back immediately if it is necessary, but never will he stop in a position where his balance will allow him to make a fast turn.

The principles throughout these instructions are focused on one final objective regarding the balance of the horse, and that is to allow

FIGS. 73, 74

him to select his own balance regardless of what the move may be. (Fig. 74) At first you will help and assist him, but as his schooling progresses, you allow him to select his own balance as he is better qualified to determine what balance is necessary for the job. A horse is not a mechanical creature, but he will react like one if treated like one.

The mechanical stop used in some of the Western divisions is indeed a poor imitation of a correct stop. Unfortunately, there are judges that accept this type of stop, and many people have ribbons and trophies to prove it, but that does not make it correct. Even to the amateur a mechanical stop is very easy to detect, as the horse's head is overbent like a Trojan horse. This is evidence that the head set was created mechanically. The horse is over the bit, the mouth wide open as the center of the mongrel spade bit rakes across the roof of his mouth; the rider's legs are stuck forward of the cinch (instead of being over the center of gravity) driving his weight through the horse's shoulders and forcing the horse's forequarters to the ground as he stops. The horse will try, in spite of his rider, to shift part of his weight to his hindquarters, and he will do this by crouching lower behind assuming a sitting position, whipping his tail furiously, indicating his discomfort, and at the same time erasing some of the evidence of his longer-than-necessary slide. In some ways this mechanical stop may look somewhat like the stop made by the roping horse, but I can assure you, it is not the same, as the roping horse selects his own balance to brace himself against the impact.

Horses, if allowed to select their own balance, will vary their stop according to the change of terrain and the job that has to be done. For instance, notice the lackadaisical stops and turns of the cutting horse, with no two stops being alike. If there is no interference from his rider, he is fully confident of his balance and of his athletic superiority to the steer he is hazing. He was simply taught to follow the movements of the steer, and some horses become experts at this, if the rider does not interfere, and manage to keep their own balance.

Watch the veteran polo pony as he makes his stops and starts if the rider allows the horse to select his own balance, assisting, of course, in whatever way the rider can, but never obstructing. You will notice the polo pony's stops will also vary in stance; sometimes he may stop with his forelegs in the air, another time he may stop using all four feet. But one thing you can be certain of, he will stop, and quickly, as he has learned to follow the ball. The rider simply works with him. There is no pulling or tugging at the bit. Just as the cutting horse follows the steer, and the veteran polo pony follows the ball, you should school your horse to follow the movements of the rider. With this thought in mind constantly correcting, never allowing the horse to refuse to yield to the pressure of the legs and thighs, in time you will have a horse that will follow his rider with the same precision that a cutting horse or well-schooled polo pony will muster.

14 / WHEELABOUTS AND ROLLBACKS

WHEN THE COLT is doing a good stop smoothly, with head well flexed and front legs off the ground, you should school him to make a fast turn. (Figs. 75, 76) This is done much the same as is the pivot on the haunches, with a few innovations. It will be done much faster with his front legs in the air, and they will remain in the air until the turn has been completed. (Fig. 77) This is started from a quick stop, while the colt's legs are still under him and your weight rests in both stirrups. Your left hand holds the head high but well flexed, and the whip is carried in your right hand. Bring the head and neck slightly to the right so that you begin to lighten the colt's left foreleg, then drop your weight to your right knee while using it and your thigh to put pressure against his shoulder. (Fig. 78) Maintain enough pressure with the calf of your right leg to keep the colt from moving his hindquarters to the right. It will be the colt's right foreleg that will start the drive to the left.

As soon as motion is indicated, bring the rein slightly up and to the left so that the colt's weight is directed to his left hind leg, at the same time rolling your weight over the saddle, bringing it to rest on the left stirrup. At first, allow the colt to bring his forefeet to the ground before jumping out again into a right lead. Always jump out into a right lead completing a rollback to the left as the colt is in the

Figs. 75, 76   The fast turn.

FIGS. 77, 78, 79, 80   The rollback. ⟶

FIG. 76

proper position to do this. A rollback to the right would be just the opposite.

After the colt has mastered this movement, you can jump him out before his front feet strike the ground on completing a rollback. (Figs. 79, 80) This is really spectacular to see when done properly. If you master this, you will have some of the feeling of unity you are seeking.

Give the colt plenty of time to grow mentally as well as physically. Do not overdo any of these collected movements, as even a well developed, mature horse cannot stand too much of this kind of work for a prolonged period. I cannot stress too emphatically the importance of having the colt do the rollback with his front legs off the ground. It could not possibly be a rollback if the colt simply ran around himself.

The horse that seems to be making a fast turn by pumping his front feet up and down as he goes around, first gives us the impression of speed. Actually, a rollback done in the air is three times as fast. These run-around horses so often seen in the show ring are usually trained by forceful methods; their bodies as well as their heads and necks are stiff, with no flexion whatsoever. They usually bear scars on their shoulders from brutal use of the spur. Tie-downs have to be used in order to keep their heads down. There are quite an assortment of torture weapons that have been devised to produce this frustrated imitation horsemanship.

Never use a spur forward of the cinch. Never kick with a spur. Use it only as instructed.

Remember, a horse is but a mirror from which his master's moods are reflected. Make these reflections honorable. (Fig. 81)

Fig. 79

Fig. 80

Fig. 81   A horse reflects his master.

15 / CONCLUSION

THE COLT'S EDUCATION has covered, so far, almost four years of schooling. The reason it has taken so long is obvious. The colt had to grow up, so we took advantage of this period of waiting to teach him what we could. There may be some who would say that it has taken much too long, that you could do it in far less time, that you should not start training until the colt is at least three years of age. Also, you would not go through all the tomfoolery that we have been busy with, that all you need do is put a good rein on him and the rest will take care of itself in time.

This is an old story. It's like the youngster who learned to play the piano with one finger. He thought he was good and his non-musical relatives thought he was wonderful. Then one day he heard a concert pianist and realized that fine piano playing was not something you could do with one finger or in a short time.

The same thing applies to training horses. It is not something that can be done easily and in a short period of time. It takes long hours of hard work and concentration. But the results will be worth it. If you continue these exercises with persistence, striving to master and perfect the training of your horse, you will be amply rewarded with a symphony of good horsemanship. When the sway and rhythm are evident, when both horse and rider seem to be governed by one brain, you will have achieved that unity of horse and man, possible only when the trainer has a genuine understanding of his animal.

144

INDEX